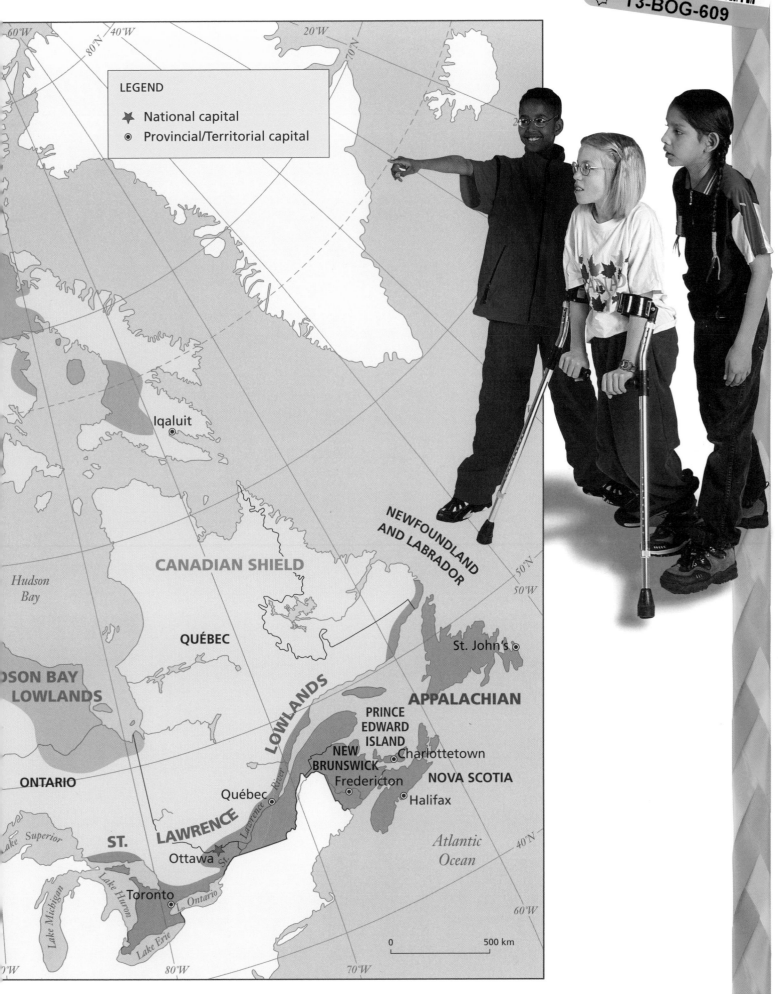

LEGEND

⭐ National capital

◉ Provincial/Territorial capital

60°W 40°W 20°W

80°N

70°W

Iqaluit ◉

CANADIAN SHIELD

NEWFOUNDLAND AND LABRADOR

50°N

50°W

Hudson Bay

QUÉBEC

St. John's ◉

DSON BAY LOWLANDS

LOWLANDS

APPALACHIAN

PRINCE EDWARD ISLAND

NEW BRUNSWICK

Charlottetown ◉

ONTARIO

NOVA SCOTIA

Québec ◉

Fredericton ◉

Halifax ◉

St. Lawrence River

Atlantic Ocean

40°N

Lake Superior

ST.   LAWRENCE

Ottawa ⭐

40°W

Lake Michigan

Lake Huron

Toronto ◉

L. Ontario

60°W

Lake Erie

80°W

70°W

0   500 km

Our Country, Canada

2nd Edition

Mary Cairo
Luci Soncin

DUVAL

Our Country, Canada 2nd Edition

Mary Cairo • Luci Soncin

Nelson Duval Project Team

Project Manager
Karen Iversen

Editors
Shauna Babiuk, Jill Fallis, Karen Iversen

Interior Design
Obsidian Multimedia Corporation,
Claudia Pompei

Photo Research
Joanne Meredith, David Strand

Production
Joanne Meredith, Jeff Miles, Leslie Stewart

Maps
Johnson Cartographics Inc., Wendy Johnson

Photographer
New Visions Photography, Brad Callihoo

Photo Shoot Coordinator
Roberta Wildgoose

Photographic Models

Francis	Eddie Chartrand
Mrs. Patel	Shellina Pirmohamed
Luke	Ethan Flett
Lincoln	Gouled Omar
Annie	Allison Iriye
Madeleine	Kay Rollans
Lorie	Jillian Oliver
Robert	Brett Zon

Copyright © 2007 by Nelson
Education Ltd.

ISBN 13: 978-1-55446-856-0
ISBN 10: 1-55446-856-6

Printed and bound in Canada
3 4 5 6   14 13 12 11

For more information, contact
Nelson Education Ltd,
1120 Birchmount Road, Toronto, Ontario
M1K 5G4. Or you can visit
our Internet site at
http://www.nelson.com

Review Team, 1st Edition

Educational
Dolores Cascone
Curriculum Resource Teacher
Toronto Catholic District School Board

Betty Goulden
Educational Consultant
Keswick, Ontario

Mary Nelson
Teacher (retired)
Calgary, Alberta
Calgary Public Board of Education

Pat Waters
Curriculum Consultant (retired)
Waterloo Catholic District School Board

Content
Dr. Bruce Rains
Department of Earth and
  Atmospheric Science
University of Alberta
Edmonton, Alberta

Bias Reviewer
John Smith
Principal
Green Glade Senior Public School
Mississauga, Ontario

ii

Acknowledgements

The authors would like to acknowledge those involved in the production of the book. We are grateful to Karen Iversen of Thomson Duval for her vision and guidance. Without her, this book would not have been created. Special thanks also go to Betty Gibbs, who tirelessly edited and patiently consulted with us throughout the writing process.

Thanks to the entire team for their many suggestions and contributions that greatly enhanced the text.

Thanks to Murray Gillespie of Winnipeg, Manitoba.

We would both like to thank our families for their understanding when time was at a premium and for their patience, support, and encouragement throughout.

Credits

Legend: b = bottom; c = centre; l = left; r = right; t = top

If not listed below, photos are by Digital Vision (cover), Digital Stock, or Corel. Photos of Francis, Luke, Annie, Lorie, Mrs. Patel, Lincoln, Madeleine, Robert, the bread basket on 40, the amythest on 64, and the fruit basket on 87, taken by New Vision Photography, Brad Callihoo. Puzzle piece, EyeWire/Getty; Post-it note icon, Books icon, PhotoSpin; Telescope icon, PhotoDisc/Getty; Provincial flags and flowers reproduced in Chapter 9 are from the Department of Canadian Heritage. Provincial birds reproduced in Chapter 9 are illustrated by John Crosby, reproduced with permission from the Canadian Museum of Nature, Ottawa, Canada.

Chapter 1. 4: both, Dan Koegler/Geovisuals 5: l, Shutterstock; r,Stephen Mcsweeny/Shutterstock 6: Worldsat International -- www.worldsat.ca --- 2001. All rights reserved. 7: (1, 2, 4, 7) Dan Koegler/Geovisuals; (5) Murray Gillespie; (6) Photos.com; (3) Raymond Gehman/National Geographic Image Collection

Chapter 2. 17: tl, tr Dan Koegler/Geovisuals 18: tl, © Paul A. Souders/ CORBIS 20: text, "And My Heart Soars," by Chief Dan George. Copyright © 1974, 1989 Hancock House Publishers Ltd., 19313 Zero Avenue, Surrey, BC.; t, Emily Carr, Above the Trees, c. 1935-1939, oil on paper, Vancouver Art Gallery, Emily Carr Trust VAG 42.3.83; b, Werner Forman/Art Resource, NY 21: tr, cr, bl, Gary Fiegehen; cl, Jared Hobbs 24: tl, Gary Vestal/Getty 25: tr, Courtesy Teck Cominco 26: b, Dan Koegler/Geovisuals; tl, Gary Fiegehen; tr, Jared Hobbs

Chapter 3. 29: b, Grasslands National Park/Brad Muir; cr, © Grandmaison Photography/www.grandmaison.mb.ca; tr, Tessa Macintosh 30: l, Grasslands National Park; r, © Grandmaison Photography/ www.grandmaison.mb.ca 32: tl, CP PHOTO/John Woods; tr, © Canada Post Corporation {1991}. Reproduced with Permission. 33: b, christine balderas/istockphoto 34: Taken from A Prairie Alphabet, illustration copyright © 1992 by Yvette Moore, published by Tundra Books. 35: Taken from A Prairie Alphabet, illustration copyright © 1992 by Yvette Moore, published by Tundra Books. 36: l, br, ©Barrett&MacKay Photo; tr, Grasslands National Park 37: tr, Courtesy Potash Corporation of Saskatchewan, Inc.; cr, Karl Naundorf/Shutterstock 38: Text from Eenie Meenie Manitoba by Robert Heidbreder. Text © 1996 Robert Heidbreder. Used by Permission of Kids Can Press Ltd., Toronto. 39: bl, Courtesy of Upper Canada Village.; cl, Jasenka Luk?a/Shutterstock; br, Michael West/Shutterstock; tl, Notman Photographic Archives, McCord Museum, Montreal.; cr, Shutterstock; tr, Thomas Sztanek/Shutterstock 40: cl, © Grandmaison Photography/www.grandmaison.mb.ca

Chapter 4. 43: cr, Flip Nicklin/Getty; tr, l, b, Tessa Macintosh 44: all, Tessa Macintosh 45: cr, ©Barrett&MacKay Photo; tr, J. Kobalenko/ Firstlight.ca; bl, Tessa Macintosh 46: text, "The Gift of the Whale," from Native American Animal Stories by Joseph Bruchac. Copyright © 1992 Fulcrum Publishing Inc., Golden, Colorado, USA. Reproduced with permission. All rights reserved. 47: © Winston Fraser/Alamy 48: t, Tessa Macintosh; br, Walrus Hunt, 1987" by Jimmy "Smith" Arnamissak, reproduced with permission of La Fédération des Coopératives du Nouveau Québec/Tookalook Native Arts 49: br, cr, B&C Alexander/First Light; brr, Martin Riedl/Photo Researchers, Inc.; tl, cll, bl, Notman Photographic Archives, McCord Museum, Montreal; cl, Werner Forman/ Art Resource, NY; cr, © Bryan & Cherry Alexander Photography/Alamy 50: cr, Tessa Macintosh; br, © Gunter Marx Photography/CORBIS; cl, © Lowell Georgia/CORBIS 52: cl, CP PHOTO/Bob Weber; tr, Courtesy

of Petro-Canada; br, © imagebroker/Alamy 53: t, Brian Summers/First Light; b, First Light 54: l, Larry MacDougal/Peter Arnold, Inc.; tr, Tessa Macintosh; br, Thomas Kitchin & Victoria Hurst/Getty

Chapter 5. 57: bl, Keith Levi/Shutterstock; tr, Lawren Harris, First Snow of Lake Superior, 1923, oil on canvas, Vancouver Art Gallery, Founders Fund VAG 50.4 (Photo: Trevor Mills) 59: br, Elena Elisseeva/ Shutterstock; cl, Getty; tl, tr, Tessa Macintosh 61: cl, ©Barrett&MacKay Photo; bl, Brian Milne/Firstlight.ca, tr, Courtesy of Manitoba Hydro.; br, Grant Black/Firstlight.ca 62: Jeff Strickler/iStockphoto 63: all, Temagami Chamber of Commerce 67: all, City of Greater Sudbury 68: present day, © Grandmaison Photography/www.grandmaison.mb.ca; tl, bl, © JK Enright/Alamy; cl, © Paul A. Souders/CORBIS

Chapter 6. 71: both, Murray Gillespie 72: tl, cl, © Grandmaison Photography/www.grandmaison.mb.ca; tr, bl, Murray Gillespie 73: br, BARTLETT, DES & JEN/National Geographic Society; cr, Jared Bell/ iShockphtoto; cl, Mike Cavaroc/Shutterstock 74: all, Murray Gillespie 75: br, Peter Van Wagner/iStockphoto; tl, iStockphoto/Brian Foltz 76: br, Richard C. Bennett/Shutterstock, cl, cr, Courtesy of Peetabeck Academy 77: l, Courtesy of Manitoba Hydro; tr, bl, © Grandmaison Photography/ www.grandmaison.mb.ca; br, Murray Gillespie 78: cl, bl, Courtesy of Manitoba; tr, Jared Bell/iStockphoto.com; r, © Grandmaison Photography/www.grandmaison.mb.ca

Chapter 7. 81: cr, ©Barrett&MacKay Photo; bl, Ron Watts/Getty 82: both, Thies Bogner/Welland 84: Thies Bogner/Welland 86: tl, Brenda McEwan/istockphoto.; cl, Victor Kapas/istockphoto.com; br, altrendo nature/Getty 87: cl, tr, Barrett & MacKay Photography Inc. 88: tr, "Envelopes" contemporary quilt by Bridget O'Flaherty, Perth, Ontario; bl, "The Road Not Taken" freeform embroidered quilt by Bridget O'Flaherty, Perth, Ontario 89: tr, CP PHOTO/Jacques Boissinot 90: bl, Bill Brooks/Alamy; t, Zoran Milich/Masterfile; br, © Jim West/Alamy

Chapter 8. 93: cl, Robert Rushton/istockphoto.com 94: all, ©Barrett&MacKay Photo 95: tr, ©Barrett&MacKay Photo; b, Photo by Boily Photo 96: all, ©Barrett&MacKay Photo 97: r, ©Barrett&MacKay Photo; l, Courtesy of Hibernia 98: tl, bl, ©Barrett&MacKay Photo; tr, christine balderas/istockphoto; cr, © Carl & Ann Purcell/CORBIS 99: text, "The Newfoundland Cod," from Don't Eat Spiders. Copyright © 1985 by Robert Heidbreder. Reproduced by permission of Fitzhenry & Whiteside Publishers, 195 Allstate Parkway, Markham, ON, L3R 4T8, Canada 100: both, Barrett & MacKay Photography Inc

Chapter 9. 104: cl, ©Barrett&MacKay Photo 109: t, Intellectual Property Program; b, calvio/istockphoto.com 110: t, Courtesy of the Yukon Executive Council; b, © Publiphoto Diffusion Inc/Alamy 111: t, Tourism, Parks, Recreation and Culture 112: b, David Prichard/First Light; t, Legislative Assembly of the NWT 113: b, © Grandmaison Photography/ www.grandmaison.mb.ca; t, Office of Protocol and Honours 114: t, Communications Services Manitoba 115: b, B&C Alexander/Firstlight.ca; t, Government of Nunavut 116: t, Communications Services Branch 117: t, © Grandmaison Photography/www.grandmaison.mb.ca; b, Stutterstock 119: t, Direction des Communications 120: t, Minister of Municipal Affairs 121: t, Communications New Brunswick 122: b, ©Barrett&MacKay Photo; t, Communications Nova Scotia 123: b, ©Barrett&MacKay Photo; t, Executive Council Office

Chapter 10. 126: cl, Courtesy of Hibernia; cr, Suzanne Tucker/ Shutterstock; tl, © Grandmaison Photography/www.grandmaison.mb.ca; tr, MCpl Armstrong of the princess Louise Fusiliers (Halifax) assist in the clean up of the camp HillCemetery in Halifax, 2003. Reproduced the permission of the Minister of Public Works and Government Services, courtesy of the Department of National Defence, 2007.; 128: cr, Courtesy TransLink 128: tr, cl, © Grandmaison Photography/www.grandmaison.mb.ca; tl, Neil Barman/istockphoto.com; tc, Sergey Vladimirovic/www.shutterstock.com; b, vera bogaerts/istockphoto. 131: tr, CP PHOTO/Aaron Harris; br, Firstlight; tl, Photodisc/Getty; bl, © Tetra Images/Alamy 134: br, ©Barrett&MacKay Photo bl, CP PHOTO/Frank Gunn; cr, CP Photo/ Kevork Djansezian; tl, © John Nakata/Corbis; tr, © Tim O'Hara/Corbis 135: bl, CP PHOTO/Ryan Remiorz; r, photo by Cylla von Tiedemann; tl, © Bryan & Cherry Alexander Photography/Alamy 136: br, Photo from NASA; t, © Thinkstock/Alamy; bl, © Larry Mulvehill/Corbis 137: tr, Nicolas Russell/Getty; bl, ©(2007) HER MAJESTY THE QUEEN IN RIGHT OF CANADA as represented by the Royal Canadian Mounted Police (RCMP). Reprinted with the permission of the RCMP. 138: r, Canadian National Exhibition 2001; bl, MCpl Armstrong of the princess Louise Fusiliers (Halifax) assist in the clean up of the camp HillCemetery in Halifax, 2003. Reproduced the permission of the Minister of Public Works and Government Services, courtesy of the Department of National Defence, 2007.

To the Student

Canada is a large and varied country. Canadians are fortunate to have many different environments in which to live. In different places, the land takes different forms. For example, some types of landforms are high mountains, wide flat plains, and rolling hills.

The surfaces of the landforms are clothed with many different types of plants. Thick forests, waving fields of grasses, rich farmlands, and bare fields of ice describe just a few different places in Canada.

The weather varies a great deal in different places. Summer weather may be hot and sweltering. The southern, more humid areas of Canada are often like that. It may be cool and sunny, as northern communities often are. Near an ocean, winter may be mild, cool, and wet. In other places, winter may be icy cold, with a whipping wind.

Canadians live in thirteen provinces and territories that are all part of the same country. The provinces and territories of Canada are connected to each other in many ways. Some examples are roads and railroads, telephone lines, and television networks. Canadians buy and sell products and provide services to other people. These are also connections.

We invite you to look at the different sides of Canada with seven student hosts and their leader, Mrs. Patel. They will help you learn how places in Canada are both similar and different. The notes, interviews, photographs, charts, and diagrams will help you understand the different environments in Canada and the people who live in them. Throughout the book, the student hosts will also introduce you to environmental issues that affect the future of our country.

Social Studies helps us learn about different places and different ways in which people live. We hope that your knowledge and appreciation of Canada will grow from working with this book.

The Canada Project

Your class will be working on a project about Canada's provinces and territories. You will learn more about the project at the end of Chapter 1.

Contents

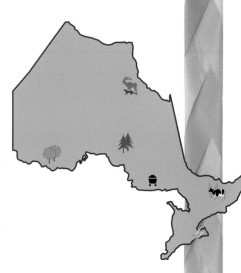

Chapter 1

Let's Look at Canada

Hello, everybody! It's wonderful to have you here. Welcome to the Chateau Laurier. It's a hotel in Ottawa, Ontario, the capital of Canada!

Seven students have been invited here to a conference to share information with you about the parts of Canada they come from. Together, we are going to build a picture of our country.

Before we do anything else, we will introduce ourselves and show you on this map where we come from. I am Mrs. Sulema Patel and I am from Ottawa. I will be leading you during this conference.

Focus on Learning

In this chapter, you will learn about
- studying our environment
- skills
- reading a satellite image
- physical regions of Canada
- reading a map
- making comparisons
- doing a research project

Vocabulary

environment
region
political region
boundary
physical region
relief map
elevation

physical
 features
landforms
climate
vegetation
natural
 resource

compass rose
cardinal
 directions
intermediate
 directions
legend
scale

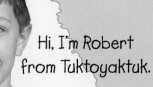

Arctic O...

Hi, I'm Robert from Tuktoyaktuk.

• Tuktoyak

YUKON

Whitehorse ⊙

NORTHW
TERRITO

*Pacific
Ocean*

BRITISH
COLUMBIA

ALBERTA

Edmont

• Lac

Nanaimo •
Victoria ⊙

Hi, I'm Annie from Nanaimo.

Hi, I'm Luke from Lacombe.

Political Map of Canada

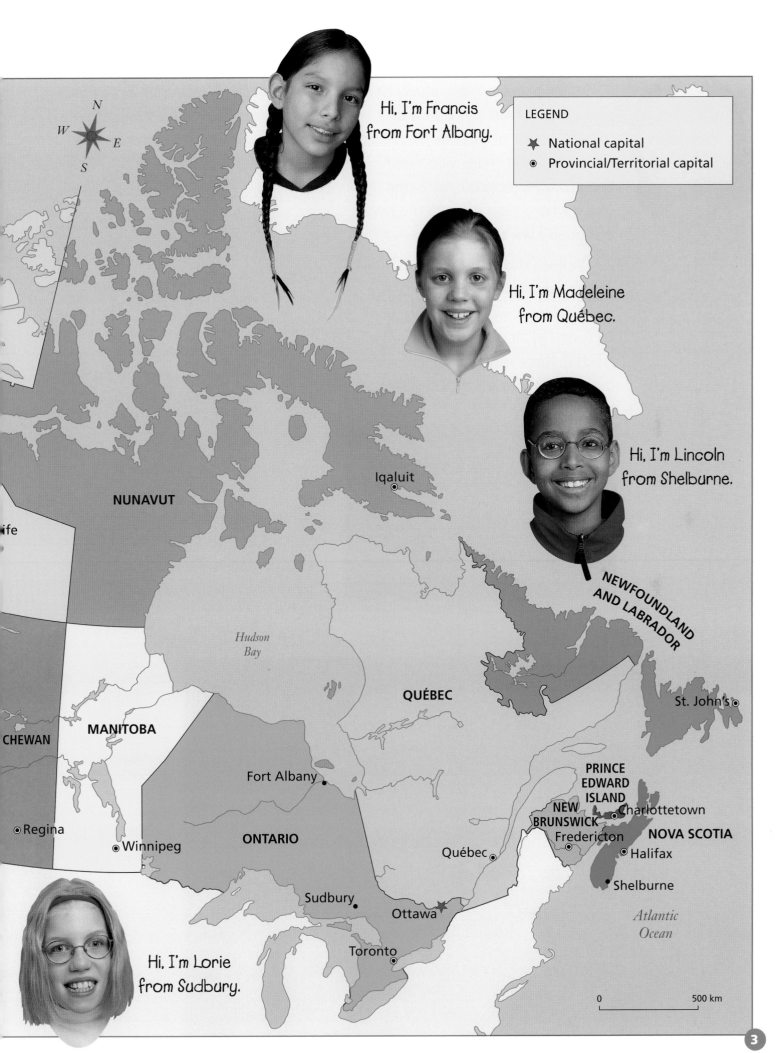

Hi, I'm Francis from Fort Albany.

Hi, I'm Madeleine from Québec.

Hi, I'm Lincoln from Shelburne.

Hi, I'm Lorie from Sudbury.

LEGEND

★ National capital
◉ Provincial/Territorial capital

NUNAVUT

Iqaluit

ife

Hudson
Bay

NEWFOUNDLAND
AND LABRADOR

QUÉBEC

St. John's ◉

MANITOBA

CHEWAN

PRINCE
EDWARD
ISLAND

NEW
BRUNSWICK

Charlottetown ◉

NOVA SCOTIA

◉ Regina

◉ Winnipeg

ONTARIO

Fort Albany ●

Québec ◉

Fredericton ◉

Halifax ◉

Shelburne ●

Atlantic
Ocean

Sudbury ●

Ottawa ★

Toronto ◉

0   500 km

3

Studying Our Environment

I am a geographer. I study the environment that surrounds us. I study how it affects us and how we also affect the environment. For example, the weather in the place where I live affects the kind of house I will build.

Choices that we make can affect our environment and other people. For example, you may want to farm the land on which you live. What if there is not enough rain or a source of water to grow strong,

healthy crops? You might dig a canal and change the way a stream flows. This would affect the environment and other people.

Skills

Special skills are used in Social Studies to learn about people, the places where they live, and their ways of life. Maps, photographs, and images are used to look at countries and landforms. Graphs, charts, and diagrams are studied to learn about people and their environments (their surroundings).

This landscape has been formed by natural forces and changed very little by people.

The straight roads, the patterns made by cutting grain fields, and the farm buildings show that this environment has been changed by people.

Regions of Canada

Canada is the second-largest country in the world. The land area is 9 017 699 square kilometres. There are thousands of lakes and thousands of kilometres of rivers.

It is difficult to look at a country as large as Canada without breaking it up into smaller parts. **Regions** are areas that are similar throughout. They are different from the areas around them. There are many types of regions. In this book, you will look at political regions and physical regions.

Two Types of Regions

A **political region** is an area with an agreed-upon boundary and its own government. A **boundary** is the outline of an area. It shows where the area begins and ends. The political regions of Canada are called *provinces* and *territories*.

A **physical region** is a part of the Earth where the environment is similar throughout and different from the regions beside it.

Coming Up
You will learn more about political regions in Chapter 9 of this book.

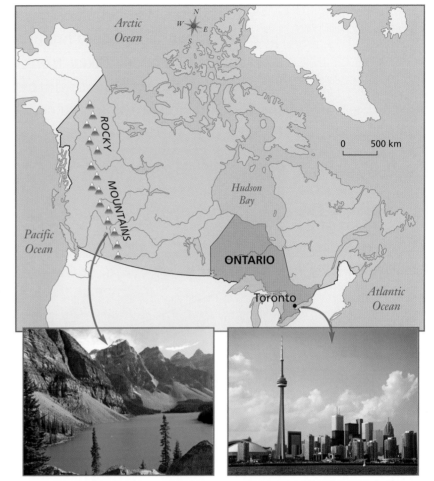

The Rocky Mountains are in a physical region. Mountains are a characteristic of the region.

Ontario is a political region. Toronto is the capital city of Ontario.

Do ◆ Discuss ◆ Discover

1. a) Working in pairs, create a list of all of the provinces and territories of Canada that you know. Write them in your notebook.
   b) How many provinces are there?
   c) How many territories are there?
   d) What is the total number of provinces and territories?

2. Use the map inside the front cover of this textbook to check your answers. Fill in any that you missed.

3. Label the provinces and territories on an outline map of Canada. Locate and label the places where the seven children come from. (Check pages 2 and 3 for these.)

Reading a Satellite Image

Satellites provide people with images of the surface of the Earth. They are taken from many hundreds of kilometres away in space. This is an image of Canada taken from a satellite. The colours are not true to life. The colours represent information that the satellite records about the Earth. Look at the image carefully. Can you find some places in Canada that you can see from a satellite?

Mountains, large bodies of water, ice, land, and the shapes of the ocean floor are recorded in this satellite image.

Satellite Image of Canada

Do ◆ Discuss ◆ Discover

1. With a partner, try to find these places on the satellite image. (You may need to use an atlas to be sure.)

   a) Pacific Ocean

   b) Atlantic Ocean

   c) Rocky Mountains

   d) Great Lakes

   e) areas of permanent ice

   f) Newfoundland and Labrador

   g) Hudson Bay

   h) St. Lawrence Seaway

2. In your notebook, describe two facts about Canada using information from the satellite image.

3. Look at the satellite image. In your notebook, write two questions you have about Canada's physical regions. These questions may help guide your learning in the following chapters.

Relief Map of Canada

A map is a drawing that shows the surface of the Earth from above. Different maps show different information about the surface of the Earth.

The map on this page is a **relief map**. A relief map shows you what land is flat and what is hilly or mountainous. All places that are certain heights above sea level are coloured the same. This shows what the surface of the land looks like. The legend of the map shows you what **elevations** are represented by each colour. Elevation is the height above sea level of a place.

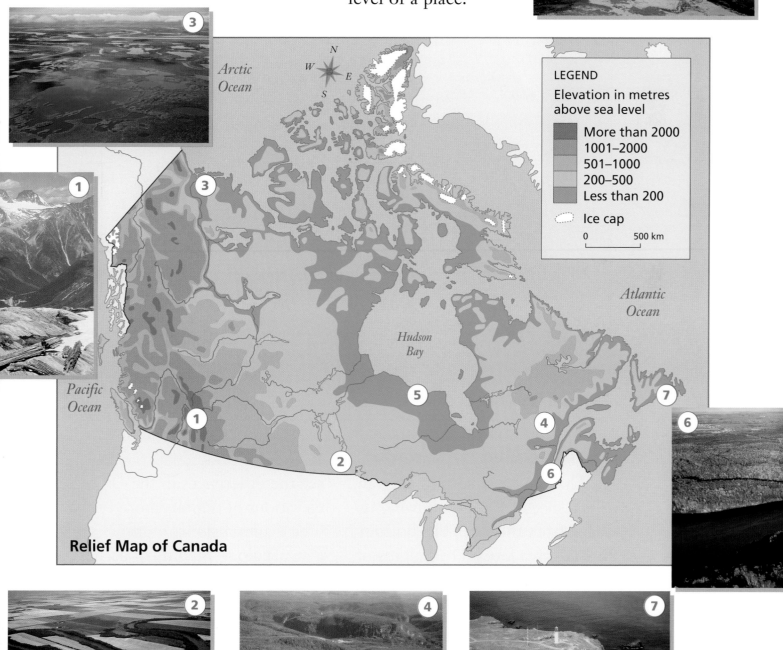

LEGEND
Elevation in metres above sea level

More than 2000
1001–2000
501–1000
200–500
Less than 200

Ice cap

0   500 km

Relief Map of Canada

Arctic Ocean

Pacific Ocean

Atlantic Ocean

Hudson Bay

Physical Regions of Canada

A physical region is a part of the Earth with a similar environment throughout that is different from the regions around it.

For example, the Canadian Shield physical region can be described as a large area of rocky hills and lakes. The Interior Plains region is a large area of nearly level ground with long rivers running through it.

Some regions have high elevation and others are close to sea level.

Coming Up
You will learn more about seven physical regions of Canada in Chapters 2 to 8.

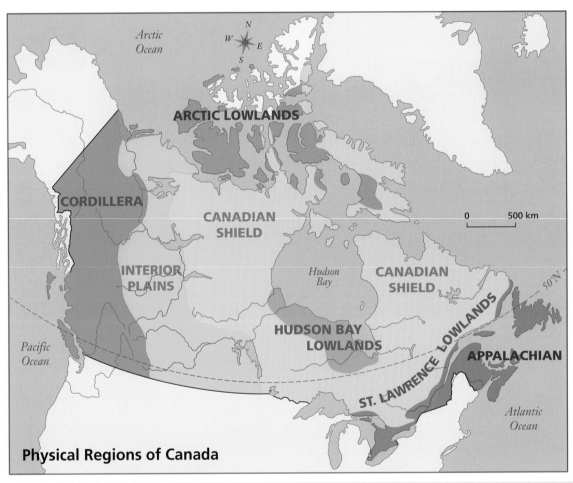

Physical Regions of Canada

Cross-Section of Canada

This is a cross-section diagram. It is a slice of Canada showing its shape from the side. The bottom line is at sea level. The heights of the mountains and hills are exaggerated. This way, you can see the differences in the elevations of regions more easily. The diagram shows a profile of Canada along the line of dashes marked on the Physical Regions of Canada map above.

Cordillera	Interior Plains	Canadian Shield	Appalachian

0   500 km

Describing Physical Regions

A physical region has similar physical features, climate, vegetation, animal life, and natural resources throughout it.

Physical features are the **landforms** and bodies of water in a place.

The highest landforms are mountains. A mountain range is a line of mountains. Valleys are low areas between mountains or hills.

Landforms that are high but flat are called plateaus. Plateaus are often found between two mountain ranges.

Hills are rounded landforms that are smaller than mountains. Plains are low flat areas. In western Canada, the large area of plains is also called the prairies.

Bodies of water include oceans, lakes, and rivers. There are many other names for special types of water bodies. For example, a sea is a body of salt water, smaller than an ocean, that is partly enclosed by land.

Climate is the average pattern of weather over many years. Temperature and precipitation (rain, snow, sleet) are both parts of climate.

Vegetation is all of the plants that naturally grow in a place. The climate of a place affects the plants that grow there. If there are few warm days, little will grow. If there is a lot of rain and warm weather, plants will grow large. If it is hot and dry, like a desert, only special desert plants will grow.

The animal life of a region includes animals, birds, fish, and other living creatures. A region beside an ocean will have both land animals and marine (water) animals.

Natural resources are materials from nature that people use to make their lives easier and more enjoyable. Some natural resources are forests, water, minerals, soil, and fish.

Reading a Map

A map is a drawing that represents the Earth's surface seen from above. A cartographer is a person whose occupation is making maps. When you make a map, there are certain parts that you must remember to add. They give information to the person who is reading the map.

Boundaries outline places. Different types of boundaries use different kinds of lines.

Lines on a map have many uses. These include boundaries, rivers, and transportation routes.

Labels name physical features and places. Physical features include rivers, oceans, deserts, mountains, and other parts of the environment. Places include countries, provinces, cities, and towns.

Physical Regions of Canada

The title tells what information is included on the map.

Lines of latitude are parallel lines that run east–west. Lines of longitude run north–south, reaching from the North Pole to the South Pole. Lines of latitude and longitude form a grid that helps locate places on the map.

A **compass rose** shows the directions on a map. A very simple compass rose just shows where north is. All maps should show north at the top of the page. Some compass roses include both the **cardinal directions** and the **intermediate directions**. The cardinal directions are north, south, east, and west. The intermediate directions are between them; for example, northwest (NW).

The **legend** of a map explains the symbols, colours, and lines used on the map.

The **scale** of a map compares a distance measured on the map with a distance on the surface of the Earth.

Colours identify areas that have something in common.

Do ◆ Discuss ◆ Discover

1. What is the title of the map on pages 10 and 11? What information does the title give? What information would a map with the title "Vegetation Regions of Canada" include?

2. Identify three different labels shown on the map.

3. What colour are the rivers and bodies of water?

4. Identify an example of a boundary on this map.

5. Look for the compass rose on this map. One intermediate direction is northwest. What do you think the others are?

6. Describe three ways in which lines are used on this map.

7. What is the symbol used to represent mountains? What other symbols are shown in the legend for this map?

Comparison

An organizer is a chart that helps show how information about something is related. Two types of organizers are described below.

A comparison chart is an organizer used to compare two or more things. It shows the ways they are the same and different. To compare two things, you must first decide what characteristics of the things are important to you. These are the comparison criteria.

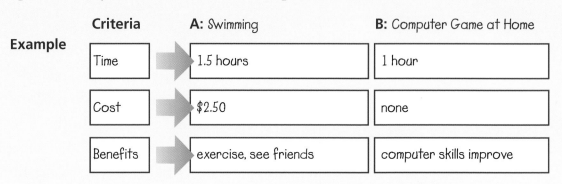

Criteria	A: Swimming	B: Computer Game at Home
Time	1.5 hours	1 hour
Cost	$2.50	none
Benefits	exercise, see friends	computer skills improve

List the criteria on your organizer. Carefully look at the two things you are comparing. Write down what you find out beside the appropriate criteria.

A Venn diagram is another way of comparing things. It is made up of two overlapping circles. In the middle space, you write the characteristics shared by both things that you are comparing. These are ways the two things are the same. In the outside parts of the circles, you write the characteristics that are different.

Example

City
- more people than a town
- highrise buildings
- malls
- hospitals

- homes
- schools
- libraries
- parks

Town
- fewer people
- no highrises
- stores
- doctors' offices

Do ◆ Discuss ◆ Discover

With a partner, do either question 1 or 2.

1. Draw a blank comparison chart organizer in your notes. Choose three criteria for comparing the satellite image on page 6 and the relief map of Canada on page 7. Complete the comparison.

2. Use a Venn diagram to compare the relief map on page 7 with the political map on pages 2 and 3.

Chapter 1

Knowledge and Understanding

1. a) Begin a vocabulary section in your notebook. Create a title page and/or a divider in your binder to mark it. Add to this section throughout your study.

   b) In pairs, look at the vocabulary presented on page 2. Use "Map" and "Region" as category words. Try to list other words under the two category words.

2. In an organizer, list the physical regions of Canada. Beside each one, identify a unique characteristic. Share your list with a partner.

3. In two or three sentences in your notebook, explain the difference between physical and political regions.

Inquiry/Research and Communication Skills

4. Look at the comparison chart or Venn diagram you created on page 12. In your notebook, write two statements about what you discovered using the organizer.

5. Find examples of three different types of maps in books, magazines, or newspapers. Examine the three maps to see if they have included the parts needed on all maps. Share your examples with a partner.

Map, Globe, and Graphic Skills

6. Create a checklist of the parts of a map to put into your notebook. You can use this checklist as a reminder every time you make a map on your own.

7. Identify, colour, and label the different physical regions of Canada on an outline map of Canada. Put this map into your notebook.

8. Create a word collage on an outline map of Canada. Think of words that describe what you have learned about Canada in this chapter and what you already knew. Write those words all over the map. Use colour and interesting lettering. Share your collage with another student.

Application

9. Create a map of your classroom. Make sure all parts of a map are included.

Internet Connection

10. Go to www.duval education.com/our countrycanada2. Click on the links to try the Canada Quiz or Word Searches.

Doing a Research Project

A major research project may be done in stages over many weeks. Often, you will work on it with a group or partner.

To do research, you must begin with a topic. Then you locate and gather information about it, organize it, and present your information.

The following steps will help you to properly complete a research project:

TOPIC

Step 1: Prepare for Research

1. Talk to your teacher to ensure that you understand exactly what you must do.

Step 2: Gather Information from Various Sources

1. Plan how your project will be organized.

2. Decide how and where to gather information. Try the library, magazines, Internet sites, and people with knowledge.

3. Record the information, keeping track of where you found it.

Step 3: Organize Your Information

1. Reread the information that you have gathered.

2. Choose the information that best applies to your topic.

3. Use charts or diagrams to help you organize your thinking.

4. Write out the information in an organized way.

Step 4: Present Your Information

1. Create materials that give information about your topic. They may be in writing, pictures, organizers, diagrams, models, objects, audio tape, or videotape.

2. Decide how you will present your materials.

3. Present your information to the rest of the class.

4. Get feedback from the class. Reflect on your project and discuss how it could have been improved.

The Canada Project

You are learning about the physical regions of Canada, the provinces and territories, and connections between parts of this country. You will be gathering, organizing, and creating materials for a class project as you learn.

There are three main parts to the project. You will work with a small group on most of it. At the end of each chapter, there is a reminder of work to do or collect for your final project.

The Scrapbook

You should include the following items in a scrapbook. You may come up with some of your own ideas as well!

- notes on the province or territory assigned to your group

- a map of the province or territory with important features and places labelled

- symbols of the resources and products of the province or territory

- poems or stories about your province or territory

- a flow chart of connections between your province or territory and other provinces and territories

- a flow chart showing the process used to create a product from a natural resource in your province or territory

- fact cards (like baseball cards) featuring key cities in your province or territory

- a map you created of your province or territory showing the major transportation routes and key cities

The Shoebox

You will collect objects, maps, fact sheets, pictures, postcards, and symbols to put into your group's shoebox. As part of the final presentation, each group will present the items in the box to the rest of the class. Your scrapbook information will help you with your presentation.

The Relief Model

Together, your class will create a large relief model of Canada. It will show the provinces and territories and the connections between them. Your teacher will help you make the pattern for your part so the model will all fit together. Each group will create a three-dimensional relief model of its province or territory. You will help put the relief model together as a class.

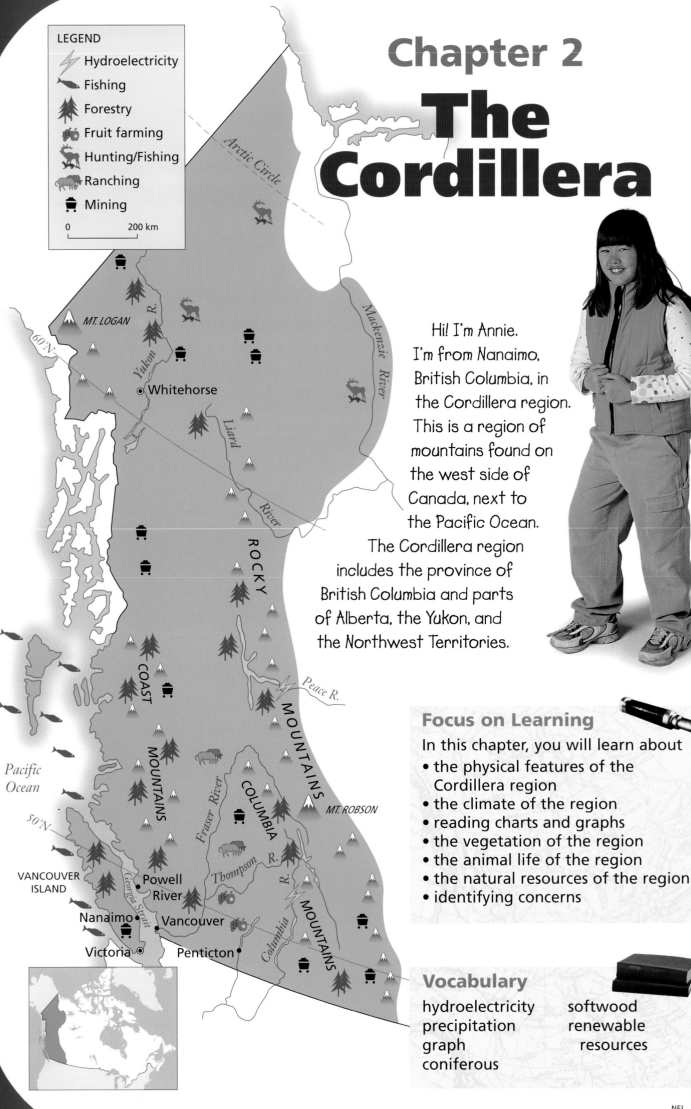

LEGEND

⚡ Hydroelectricity
🐟 Fishing
🌲 Forestry
🍇 Fruit farming
🦌 Hunting/Fishing
🦬 Ranching
⛏ Mining

0   200 km

Arctic Circle

MT. LOGAN

60°N

Yukon R.

⊙ Whitehorse

Liard River

Mackenzie River

ROCKY

Peace R.

MOUNTAINS

COAST

MOUNTAINS

Pacific
Ocean

50°N

Fraser River

COLUMBIA

R.

MT. ROBSON

Thompson R.

R.

MOUNTAINS

VANCOUVER
ISLAND

Powell
River

Georgia Strait

Nanaimo ●

Vancouver

Victoria ⊙

Penticton ●

Columbia R.

MOUNTAINS

Chapter 2
The Cordillera

Hi! I'm Annie.
I'm from Nanaimo,
British Columbia, in
the Cordillera region.
This is a region of
mountains found on
the west side of
Canada, next to
the Pacific Ocean.
The Cordillera region
includes the province of
British Columbia and parts
of Alberta, the Yukon, and
the Northwest Territories.

Focus on Learning

In this chapter, you will learn about
• the physical features of the
  Cordillera region
• the climate of the region
• reading charts and graphs
• the vegetation of the region
• the animal life of the region
• the natural resources of the region
• identifying concerns

Vocabulary

hydroelectricity   softwood
precipitation   renewable
graph   resources
coniferous

Physical Features

Millions of years ago, huge folds of rock pushed up to form mountain ranges called the Cordillera. The folds bent and crushed against each other.

The Cordillera region today has many different landforms. There are mountains, hills, plateaus, and valleys. Most of the region is high above sea level.

There are lakes of all sizes and major river systems. The Pacific Ocean lies along the western coast.

The interior plateau lies between the Columbia Mountains and the Coast Mountains. Several large rivers flow across this high country. Then they flow through the Coast Mountains to the ocean.

Mount Robson is the highest peak in the Rocky Mountains. It is 3954 metres high.

A narrow passage of water connecting two larger bodies of water is called a strait.

The interior plateau is fairly flat or has small hills.

Do ◆ Discuss ◆ Discover

Look at the map of the Cordillera region on the previous page to answer these questions. Write your answers in your notebook.

1. Which range of mountains is found along the coastline?
2. Which range of mountains is the farthest away from the coast?
3. What body of water is found between Vancouver Island and the mainland?
4. Name two rivers shown on the map.

The Cordillera region has several mountain ranges. The highest mountains in Canada are found there.

Rivers – Gifts of Nature

Many tourists visit this site on the Fraser River to watch the migration of salmon.

The Fraser River is part of the largest river system in the Cordillera region. A river system is made up of all the parts of a river and the other rivers and streams that flow into it. The Fraser River begins high in the Rocky Mountains near Jasper National Park, flows through the Coast Mountains, and empties into the Pacific Ocean.

The Fraser River system is the habitat of salmon as well as many other fish. Salmon migrate up the Fraser River and to its tributaries to spawn (lay their eggs) at more than 150 different sites.

The Life Cycle of Salmon

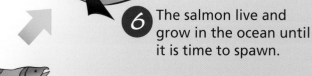

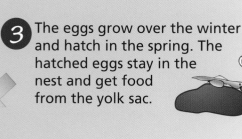

1 In the fall, the adult salmon begin their journey to spawn.

2 The salmon dig out a nest, lay the eggs, and cover them with gravel for protection against their enemies. Then most adult salmon die.

3 The eggs grow over the winter and hatch in the spring. The hatched eggs stay in the nest and get food from the yolk sac.

4 When the salmon have grown a few centimetres, they feed in streams that are close by.

5 When they are strong enough and fast enough to swim and avoid their enemies in rushing water, they begin to swim to the ocean.

6 The salmon live and grow in the ocean until it is time to spawn.

Do ◆ Discuss ◆ Discover

1. In a small group, brainstorm some changes that might harm the river habitat of the salmon.

2. With a partner, discuss why it is important to take care of the rivers and lakes.

3. Discuss with your family how caring for the waterways will help everyone. Explain two of your reasons in your notebook.

The Power of Water

The force of falling water can be used to produce electricity. This is called **hydroelectricity**.

Sometimes, a dam is built across a river to help make the electricity. A generating station is built at the bottom of the dam. Water collects in a large reservoir created by the dam and then shoots through a pipe to the turbine below. A turbine is a special type of water wheel.

When the water hits the blades of the turbine, it starts to turn. When the turbine starts moving, it turns a generator and electricity is produced. Then the water leaves the generating station and goes back into the main stream of the river.

Hands On!

Work with a partner to create a water wheel that can lift a small weight.

You will need

- a foil pie plate
- scissors
- a pencil
- tape
- a source of running water
- a piece of string 45 cm long
- a small weight (for example, a nut or a bolt)

1. Carefully cut out the circular bottom of the pie plate. Make eight equally spaced cuts towards the centre of the foil plate. End each cut about 2 cm from the centre.

2. Fold one edge of each section of the plate to form a small ledge.

3. Push a pencil through the middle of the plate. Make sure the pencil fits snugly in the hole. Tape it to the plate.

4. Tie one end of the string around the pencil (near the end). Attach the weight to the other end of the string. Now you have a water wheel.

5. Hold the wheel under the running water. Position it so the water hits the blades. Let the pencil rest lightly between your thumbs and index fingers. The wheel should wind the string around the pencil and lift the weight.

6. Try running the water over the wheel at different speeds and see what happens.

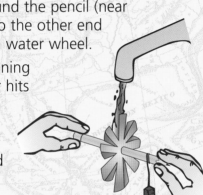

Do ◆ Discuss ◆ Discover

1. Discuss the following questions with a classmate.
   a) What happens when you run a little water over the plate?
   b) What happens when you run more water over the plate?
   c) What happens to the weight when you run water over the plate?

2. In your notebook, write a conclusion about how moving water can create energy.

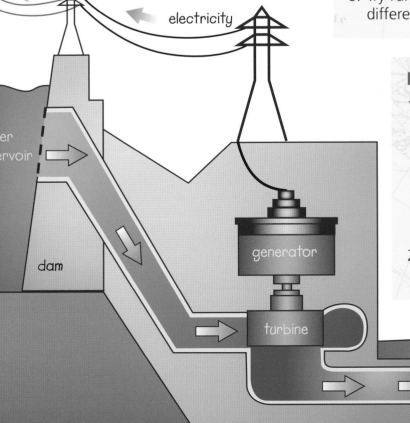

electricity

reservoir

dam

generator

turbine

back to river

Cordillera Arts

And My Heart Soars

The beauty of the trees,
The softness of the air,
The fragrance of the grass,
Speaks to me.

The summit of the mountain,
The thunder of the sky,
The rhythm of the sea,
Speaks to me.

The faintness of the stars,
The freshness of the morning,
The dewdrop on the flower,
Speaks to me.

The strength of fire,
The taste of salmon,
The trail of the sun,
And the life that never
goes away,

They speak to me.
And my heart soars.

— Chief Dan George

Emily Carr was a painter. She created beautiful images of the environment of British Columbia, such as this painting called *Above the Trees*.

This argillite stone chest was carved by Charles Edenshaw in the late 1800s. Can you see the raven in the carving?

Do ◆ Discuss ◆ Discover

1. a) What does the poet tell you about the Cordillera region in "And My Heart Soars"?

   b) Why do you think he says that everything speaks to him?

2. Describe how the work of each artist on this page represents the Cordillera region.

Climate

The climate of a place is the pattern of its weather over a long period of time. It includes both temperature and **precipitation**. Precipitation is moisture that falls as rain, snow, or sleet.

The Cordillera region has many different climates. The northern Cordillera region has cold winters and warm summers. It gets about 200 millimetres to 400 millimetres of precipitation per year.

The southern part of the region has warmer temperatures. The area along the coast has mild and rainy weather. Precipitation can be as much as 2000 millimetres per year. The ocean helps to keep places near the coast cooler in summer and warmer in winter.

Heavy snowfalls are common in mountain forests.

Grasses and flowers grow on this sunny mountainside.

The mountains and valleys of the interior plateau get hot in the summer. They can be quite cold in the winter.

The Pacific Coast is well known for frequent rain and fog.

Do ◆ Discuss ◆ Discover

Discuss the following questions with a partner.

1. Which places in the Cordillera region do you think get more rain—places near the coast or places in the interior? Which do you think get more snow? Why?

2. How are the environments in the photos on this page similar to, or different from, where you live?

Reading Charts and Graphs

Charts and **graphs** are organized ways to display information. The title of a chart or graph tells you what information is being shown. The way a chart or graph is organized helps show how the information is related. In the example below, the information is organized by year.

Many charts are used to display numbers. Numbers are also called statistics. The numbers in the chart below represent Primary Forest Production Permits for round wood. Round wood includes wood for saw logs and building logs.

Primary Forest Production Permits

Year	2000	2001	2002	2003	2004
Number of Permits	35 000	29 000	17 000	22 000	52 000

The same information can be displayed in more than one way. A graph is a visual way of showing information. It uses pictures or lines to represent numbers.

In a picture graph, each picture represents a certain amount. The legend shows how much each picture represents. In the example below, 10 000 permits are represented by one tree.

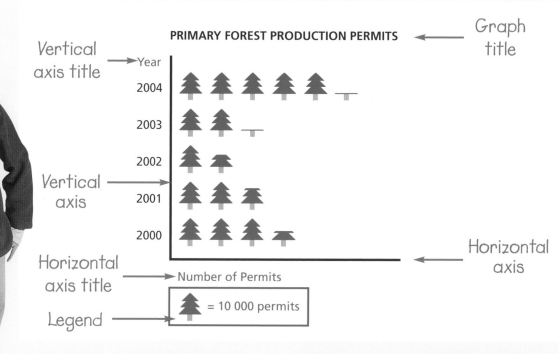

On a bar graph, the amounts are shown on a scale marked in units up the side. An example of a bar graph is shown on the next page. A bar graph may give information about one thing, or it may compare two or more things.

Comparing Climates

When you compare the climates of places, you compare their average temperatures and precipitation.

Temperature

The community of Powell River is on the coast of British Columbia. The community of Penticton is farther south in BC than Powell River. (See the map on page 16.) Use the two charts on the right to study the average temperatures for these two places.

Precipitation

Places near an ocean usually get more precipitation.

The graph on the right is a bar graph. It compares the average precipitation in winter for Powell River and Penticton. The amounts are represented by bars.

Powell River, BC – Average Temperature in Degrees Celsius											
JAN	FEB	MAR	APR	MAY	JUNE	JULY	AUG	SEPT	OCT	NOV	DEC
4	5	7	10	13	16	18	18	16	11	7	4

Penticton, BC – Average Temperature in Degrees Celsius											
JAN	FEB	MAR	APR	MAY	JUNE	JULY	AUG	SEPT	OCT	NOV	DEC
−2	1	5	9	14	17	20	20	15	9	3	−1

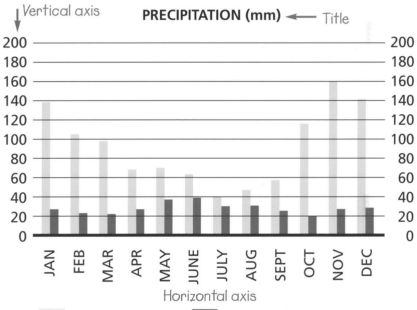

Vertical axis   PRECIPITATION (mm) ← Title

Horizontal axis

◻ Powell River, BC   ◼ Penticton, BC

Go to www.duvaleducation.com/ourcountrycanada2. Click on the link to Statistics to find out more about Canada.

Do ◆ Discuss ◆ Discover

Look at the average temperature and precipitation for each season of the year for each community.

1. Which place is warmer in the summer?

2. Which place gets the most rainfall in the summer?

3. During which months is the difference in precipitation 100 millimetres or more?

4. Why is the word *precipitation* used when describing climate, instead of just using the word *rain*?

Vegetation

The cool, rainy climate along the Pacific coast is perfect for the giant trees that grow there. Most forests of the Cordillera region are **coniferous**. Coniferous trees have needles and cones. Most coniferous trees are evergreen.

The rain forest near the Pacific Coast has the largest coniferous trees in Canada.

Most plants, shrubs, and trees grow larger on the coast than they do elsewhere. Flowering plants produce large, healthy blooms.

Mountain valleys of the Cordillera region and some parts of the interior plateau are covered in forests. The tops of the high mountains have little vegetation. There is little soil there and fewer warm days than in the valleys.

The natural vegetation of much of the interior plateau is grasses. Many other plants grow in places where rivers and lakes provide more water.

Animal Life

Many kinds of animals live on the land and in the air and water of the Cordillera region. Large parts of the region have few people in them. There is a lot of food for animal life.

The land areas are home to black bears, grizzly bears, deer, elk, lynx, cougars, and wolves. Many small animals, such as squirrels and rabbits, also live in the region. Canada geese, eagles, ravens, and owls are just a few of the birds in the region.

Polar bears and caribou are found in the far northern parts of the Cordillera region.

The Pacific Ocean is home to many kinds of sea life. The Pacific salmon is an important food resource. Marine animals, such as whales and seals, are common along the coast of the region.

A bald eagle catches a salmon near Vancouver Island.

This huge sea lion seems clumsy on shore, but it is an excellent, graceful swimmer in the ocean.

Natural Resources

The thickest forests and largest trees in Canada grow in the Cordillera region. Forest resources provide the most important products in this region.

Softwood is timber that comes from coniferous trees. It is used to make pulp and paper products. Softwood is also used in construction. Approximately 90% of the Canadian timber sold is softwood.

Approximately 45% of the copper mined in Canada comes from the Cordillera region.

Forests are a renewable resource because they can be regrown.

Trees are made into many products such as paper, plywood, cellophane, cardboard cartons, and furniture.

There are two giant hydroelectric dams on rivers in the Cordillera region. They are the Revelstoke Dam on the Columbia River and the W.A.C. Bennet Dam on the Peace River. The energy of falling water is used to create electricity.

This region has many minerals. At one time, people came from all over to search for gold in the Fraser River valley and in the Klondike River area. Gold, coal, copper, asbestos, zinc, silver, lead, sand, and gravel are mined in the region. Minerals mined there are sold all over Canada and the world.

The Pacific Ocean and the rivers and lakes are the source of many kinds of fish. Salmon, halibut, herring, and shellfish are important resources in the Cordillera region.

The Okanagan Valley in the southern part of this region has good soil and a warm climate. It is famous for its orchards. Apples, pears, plums, cherries, peaches, apricots, and grapes are produced there.

Lumber and pulp to make paper are sold to countries all over the world.

This huge vehicle is working in an open-pit copper mine, the Highland Valley mine near Kamloops, BC.

Hot summers are important for fruit crops.

Go to www.duvaleducation.com/ourcountrycanada2. Click on the link to Geographic Games to learn more about Canada.

Annie's Concern

My mother is a Royal Canadian Mounted Police constable. She is often called to work with the Ministry of Natural Resources. They sometimes ask her to enforce laws controlling how and when forests are cut. I think this is an important part of what my mother does.

I believe our forests are important to the environment. Many animals, birds, plants, and other forms of life live in them.

The forest is their habitat. If forests are cut down completely, these living things may also disappear.

I am concerned that forests are being cut down without enough planning and care for the future of our environment.

Do ◆ Discuss ◆ Discover

1. Forests are an important resource. What are three ways people can care for Canada's forests?

2. The forest provides many jobs. Brainstorm what jobs are involved in the forest industry and in caring for the forests.

3. What are some ideas, images, and words you might include on a poster to promote healthy forests?

Chapter 2

Knowledge and Understanding

1. Copy the following organizer into your notebook. First, put a title on the organizer. Name the physical region you are describing. Fill in every area with information that you have learned from this chapter and your notes.

Physical Region:	
TOPICS	WHAT I LEARNED
Physical Features	
Climate	
Vegetation	
Animal Life	
Natural Resources	

Example

2. Identify vocabulary from this chapter to add to the vocabulary section of your notebook. Draw diagrams or sketches to help you remember the words and their meanings.

Inquiry/Research and Communication Skills

3. With a partner, research jobs in the forestry industry. Follow the research model on page 14. Design a Help Wanted poster for one of the jobs you have learned about. Choose images or design ideas for getting people's attention and persuading them to apply.

Map, Globe, and Graphic Skills

4. Create your own picture symbols to show the natural resources found in the Cordillera region. Place them on an outline map of the region. Include a legend.

Application

5. Imagine you are moving to the Cordillera region. Write an e-mail or a letter describing how you feel about moving there and what you are looking forward to.

The Canada Project

1. Locate and decorate a shoebox. You will use it to hold objects, maps, and other things your group collects or makes throughout your project. Make it bright, fun, and interesting! Do the same thing with the cover of your group's scrapbook.

2. Begin a map of Canada. On an outline map of Canada, colour the Cordillera region. Label the provinces/territories that are in the Cordillera region. Add important information about the Cordillera region to your map. (Use the maps on page 16 and inside the front and back covers of the text to help.) You will be adding to your map as you work through Chapters 3 to 8.

3. Use an atlas to locate a major river that flows through your group's province/territory. Using a diagram, show the uses of the river.

Chapter 3
The Interior Plains

Hi! I'm Luke. I come from Lacombe, Alberta, in the Interior Plains region. This region stretches along the east side of the Cordillera region as far north as the Arctic Ocean. It includes the western part of the Northwest Territories and large parts of Alberta, Saskatchewan, and Manitoba.

Focus on Learning

In this chapter, you will learn about
- the physical features of the Interior Plains region
- the climate of the region
- reading images
- the vegetation of the region
- the animal life of the region
- the natural resources of the region
- identifying concerns

Vocabulary

glacier   fertile
irrigation   erosion
deciduous   harvest
wetlands

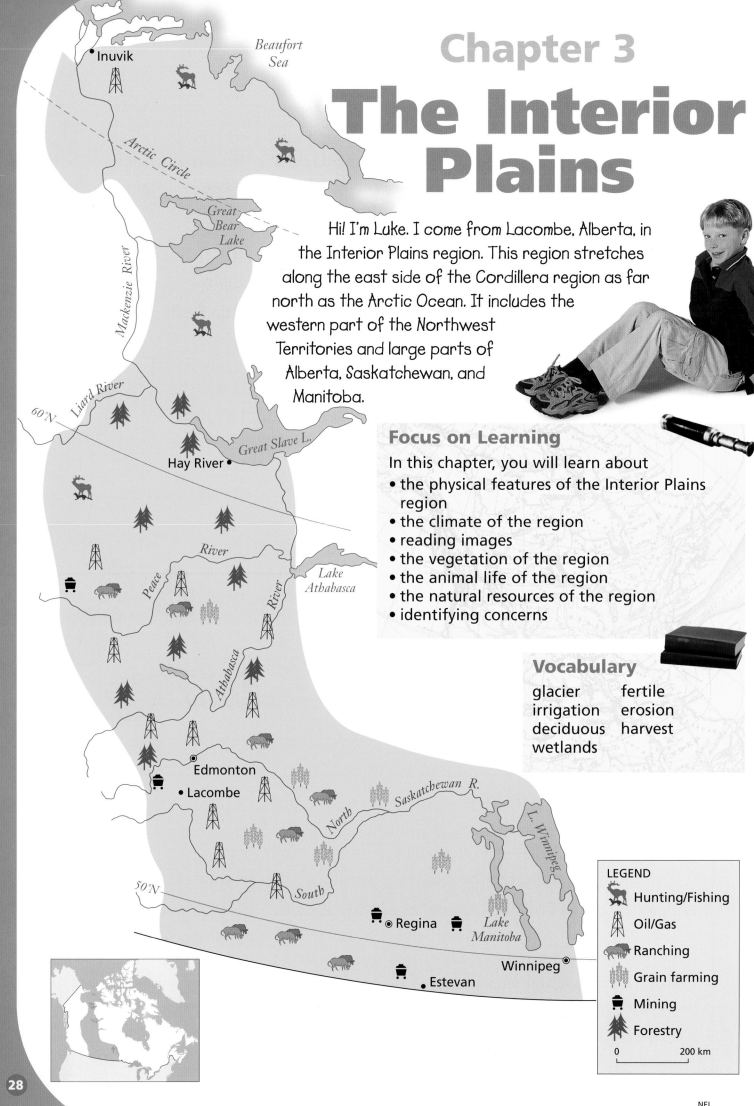

Inuvik

Beaufort Sea

Arctic Circle

Great Bear Lake

Mackenzie River

Liard River

60°N

Great Slave L.

Hay River

River

Peace River

Athabasca River

Lake Athabasca

Edmonton

Lacombe

North Saskatchewan R.

South

50°N

Regina

Lake Manitoba

Estevan

Winnipeg

L. Winnipeg

LEGEND
 Hunting/Fishing
 Oil/Gas
 Ranching
 Grain farming
 Mining
 Forestry

0   200 km

Physical Features

The Interior Plains region is nearly flat or has rolling hills. This huge plain descends in several levels. It is highest in the foothills of the Rocky Mountains. It is almost at sea level in Manitoba and the Northwest Territories.

About 18 000 years ago, much of Canada was covered by two huge sheets of ice. They were up to two kilometres thick in places. These **glaciers** grew very slowly as the whole Earth became cooler.

The weight of the glaciers caused the land to sink down. As the glaciers melted, huge lakes and rivers were formed. The lakes became smaller, but many remained. Rocks, gravel, sand, and silt were left behind. They formed hills and flat areas of plains.

Grasslands National Park in southwestern Saskatchewan was created to preserve the original prairie vegetation.

Several large lakes are found in the northern Interior Plains region.

This region has many of the largest lakes and longest rivers in Canada. Several river systems begin in the Rocky Mountains. They flow north and east to the Arctic Ocean and Hudson Bay.

The lowest, flattest parts of the Interior Plains region are the delta of the Mackenzie River and southern Manitoba.

Rivers in flat country have difficulty carrying away water because there is little downhill slope. Therefore, these flat lands often flood.

Climate

The climate of the Interior Plains region is more severe than the climate of the Cordillera region. Most places have cold winters and hot summers.

Winter in the Interior Plains region can be extremely cold, with clear sunny skies.

The Interior Plains region has less precipitation than most other regions of Canada. Places sometimes have no rain for long periods. This is called a drought.

Healthy crops need both sun and precipitation.

Latitude

The temperature of a place is affected by where it is found on the Earth. In Canada, the farther north a place is, the colder it usually is. There are few hours of daylight in winter. The Sun gives little heat. You can describe how far north a place is by saying what line of latitude it lies on.

Lines of latitude are imaginary parallel lines around the Earth. A line of latitude joins points that are equal distances from the equator. Lines of latitude are numbered in degrees N and degrees S, for north and south of the equator.

Most of the southern border of Canada is formed by the latitude line 49 degrees north (49° N). There are 90 degrees between the equator and the North Pole. All of Canada is over halfway to the North Pole. No wonder it gets cold in winter!

The symbol for degrees is °. It is used both for angles and for temperatures.

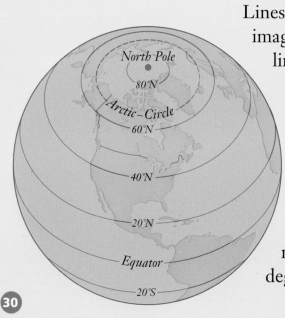

North Pole
80°N
Arctic Circle
60°N
40°N
20°N
Equator
20°S

Do ◆ Discuss ◆ Discover

1. a) Looking at a globe, describe where Canada is located compared to the equator.
   b) Middle Island, just off Pelee Island in Ontario, is the southernmost point in Canada. Estimate its latitude by looking at the globe on the left.

30

NEL

What's the Weather?

Temperature

The temperature of places in the Interior Plains region is affected by their position of latitude. The graph below compares temperatures in Estevan, Saskatchewan, and Hay River, Northwest Territories. (See the map on page 28.)

AVERAGE TEMPERATURE IN DEGREES CELSIUS

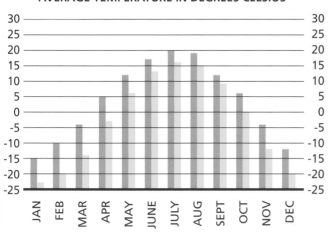

Estevan, SK   Hay River, NT

Precipitation

Regina, Saskatchewan, and Powell River, British Columbia, are both located near 50° N latitude. However, their climates are very different. In Regina, the average yearly precipitation is 378 millimetres. This is an average of 32 millimetres each month. Look at the graph on page 23 to see the precipitation in Powell River. The following illustration compares the average monthly precipitation. Powell River has more precipitation because it is nearer to the ocean.

Powell River   **Regina**

Do ◆ Discuss ◆ Discover

1. In your atlas, look up the latitudinal positions of Estevan and Hay River. One is much farther north. What is the difference between the two latitudes?

2. In your notebook, draw two thermometers side by side. On them, show the difference between Estevan's average temperatures in July and in January. Write one or two sentences under the thermometers describing the difference.

3. Compare the temperatures for Hay River and Estevan in April, May, and June. Which place is colder? What might explain the difference?

Hands On!

Work with a group to explore how rain happens. Ask an adult to help you with this activity.

You will need

- a large pot of water
- ice cubes
- a burner or stove top
- a small pot
- your notebook

1. Wait until the water in the large pot is boiling. Then place the ice into the smaller pot.

2. Hold the smaller pot over the large pot.

3. Watch the steam from the boiling water condense into liquid on the outside of the smaller pot.

4. When enough steam has condensed and the drops become heavy enough, they will fall into the large pot.

5. Draw diagrams in your notebook of what happened during each step of this activity. Explain your diagrams in writing.

Alberta Clipper

When the weather reporter says an Alberta clipper is on the way, it means it is time to hurry and bundle up. These winter storms develop east of the Rocky Mountains and quickly move across southern Canada. An Alberta clipper brings snow and much colder Arctic air with strong winds. The winds cause the snow to blow around and drift.

On October 31, 1999, an Alberta clipper whipped through Saskatchewan with winds reaching 110 kilometres per hour in Regina and 70 kilometres per hour in Saskatoon. The strong winds knocked down trees, damaged homes, and moved parked cars.

Chinook

A chinook is a warm, dry wind that blows east down the Rocky Mountains to the prairies. A chinook forms when warm, moist air climbs up the west side of the mountains. As it rises, it cools and loses moisture in the form of snow or rain. The dry air goes over the mountains and moves quickly down the east side, warming up as it goes. The air warms up almost twice as fast as it cools down!

A chinook can cause the temperature to rise very quickly. It is sometimes called "snow eater" because the warm, dry air moves so fast (up to 120 kilometres per hour) and makes the snow disappear in a short period of time. Chinook winds can last less than one hour or for a few days.

An Alberta Clipper causes the snow to blow around and drift.

This Canada Post stamp is called *Warm Wind Chinook.*

How a Chinook Forms

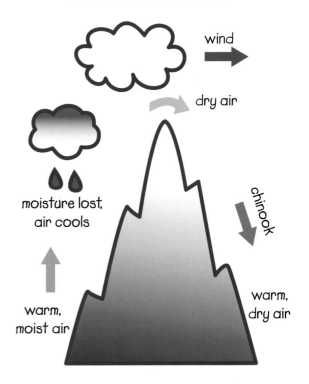

Some of the most extreme temperature changes have taken place in Pincher Creek, Alberta. On January 27, 1962, the temperature went from –18.9° C to +3.3° C in one hour. On January 6, 1966, the temperature rose 37.8° C in four minutes. That was a record!

Chinook winds sometimes come with a cloud formation called a chinook arch.

A chinook arch is made up of a band of thick clouds. Under the clouds, a large strip of sky can be seen over the Rockies. The cloud wall looks like heavy storm clouds, but rarely produces any moisture. The clouds appear to be rolling because of the movement of the air that is produced as they move over the mountainside, but the clouds do not actually move eastward.

The colours in the chinook arch are often spectacular and change throughout the day.

Ranchers watch a chinook arch in the sky.

Big Blows in Central Canada

Nation-wide January Heat Wave

BC's Long Wet and Long Dry

Prairie Hailers and a Deadly Twister

Do ◆ Discuss ◆ Discover

1. Pick one of the weather headlines above and write a news story to go with the headline.

Reading Images

When you do research, you gather information from many sources. Images are one important source of information. All kinds of pictures are images. Photographs and visual arts, such as paintings, drawings, and sculptures, are all images.

An artist chooses what is shown in an image. Everything that appears is there for a reason. When you "read" an image, first decide what you think its subject is. Then look at the details. Decide what the details tell you about the subject. Think about why they have been included in the image.

Look at the foreground for information. The subject of the image is often in the foreground. The most important parts of the picture are usually larger, clearer, and in the middle. They catch your attention.

Look at the middle ground and the background. These show where the subject is located. They give information about the surroundings or the environment.

Images usually give you a feeling about the subject.

Illustration by Yvette Moore for *A Prairie Alphabet* by Jo Bannatyne-Cugnet

Plains Arts

Illustration by Yvette Moore for *A Prairie Alphabet* by Jo Bannatyne-Cugnet

Do ◆ Discuss ◆ Discover

1. What is the subject of each image on pages 34 and 35?

2. Describe the middle ground and background of each image.

3. Describe what you see in each image and how it makes you feel.

4. a) Draw a web for each image. Identify things in the image that represent the environment of the Interior Plains region.

   b) Choose one of the images. Create a story web or a plot sequence for this image. Place the organizer into your notebook. If the Interior Plains region is part of your province or territory, you can include the organizer in your scrapbook or shoebox.

Vegetation

The natural vegetation of most of the southern Interior Plains region is grasses. When there is drought, the grasses go brown and dormant. This means they wait until there is rain before putting up new green shoots. **Irrigation** is used to bring water to crops in some dry areas.

Trees and shrubs grow along streams and near bodies of water. They are not as large as trees in the Cordillera region. Most of these trees are **deciduous**. They lose their leaves and become dormant in winter. New leaves grow in spring when water is more plentiful.

Elk Island National Park in Alberta preserves both the natural vegetation of the region and this bison herd.

In the far northern parts of the Interior Plains region, the winter is cold and the summer is very short. Only small plants, grasses, and mosses grow. There are no trees.

Animal Life

The grasslands, forests, and the northern plains are habitats for many animals, birds, and other forms of life.

Migratory waterfowl, such as these ducks, travel long distances to spend different seasons in different places.

Deer, antelope, elk, moose, and caribou are herbivores. They live on grasses, shrubs, and other vegetation.

Antelope herds are found in Grasslands National Park.

Carnivores are meat-eating animals that hunt other animals. Some carnivores in the southern part of the plains are coyotes, hawks, and eagles. Wolves and polar bears live in the north.

Ducks, geese, swans, and other waterfowl spend the summer in the northern part of the region. In the autumn, they migrate in huge flocks. They stop in grain fields on the plains and **wetlands** to feed and rest on their long journey. Wetlands are places that are marshy or partly flooded all year round.

Natural Resources

There are important mineral resources and oil and gas fields below the surface of the Interior Plains region. Large amounts of coal and potash are mined in the region. Huge fields of crude oil and natural gas are found far underground. Gas and oil are produced by drilling deep into the Earth.

The largest area of farmland in Canada is found in the southern part of the region. The soil is considered **fertile**. It contains a good mixture of materials that grow healthy plants. Cereal grains, such as wheat, oats, barley, and rye, grow well on the plains. Cereal grains are all types of grasses whose seeds are used as food.

Potash is an important ingredient in fertilizer. Saskatchewan has the largest potash industry in the world.

Grain products and oil and natural gas from the Interior Plains region are sold in Canada and around the world.

Soils

Soils are materials on the surface of the Earth in which plants can grow. They are made of pieces of finely ground rock mixed with decaying plant and animal materials. Plants grow in the top layer, called topsoil.

In most places, soils are only a thin layer on top of the bedrock of the Earth. Soil takes thousands of years to form naturally. That is why soil **erosion** is a problem. When topsoil is carried away by water, wind, or ice, or stripped off by machinery, it can take thousands of years to form new soil.

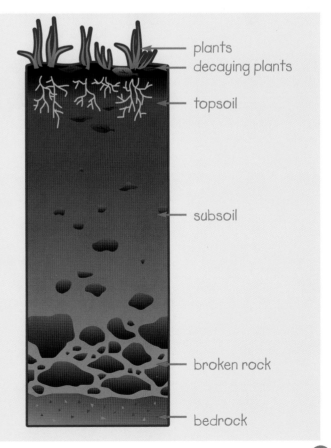

plants
decaying plants
topsoil
subsoil
broken rock
bedrock

From Harvest to Sale

An exchange of goods between two regions occurs many times between harvesting a resource and selling a finished product made from the raw materials. This flow chart shows one sequence from **harvest** to sale.

The word *harvest* is often used to describe the collecting stage of certain industries. Farming, fishing, and lumbering are three examples.

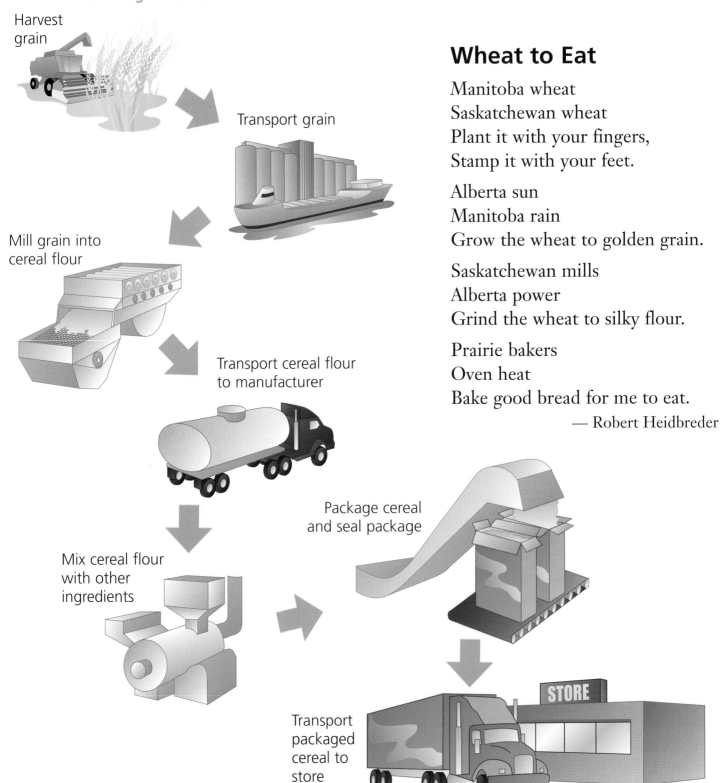

Making Breakfast Cereal

Harvest grain

Transport grain

Mill grain into cereal flour

Transport cereal flour to manufacturer

Mix cereal flour with other ingredients

Package cereal and seal package

Transport packaged cereal to store

Wheat to Eat

Manitoba wheat
Saskatchewan wheat
Plant it with your fingers,
Stamp it with your feet.

Alberta sun
Manitoba rain
Grow the wheat to golden grain.

Saskatchewan mills
Alberta power
Grind the wheat to silky flour.

Prairie bakers
Oven heat
Bake good bread for me to eat.

— Robert Heidbreder

Technology – Past and Present

Tools and machinery used in grain farming have changed and improved over the centuries. These changes have also improved the lives of present-day farmers.

PAST **PRESENT**

Do ◆ Discuss ◆ Discover

1. Using the photographs and what you already know, describe how technology has changed farm life.

2. If possible, ask a farmer to describe how technology has changed rural life. Illustrate this change in your notebook.

Luke's Concern

I live with my family on a farm near Lacombe, Alberta. Most of the wheat in Canada is grown in the southern part of the Interior Plains region. Other types of grain, such as rye, oats, and barley, are also grown there.

Many grain farmers use fertilizer and pesticides. They can increase the amount of grain the land will yield. However, pesticides and fertilizer can be washed into streams. They go into the underground water supply.

Some farmers are afraid of damaging the environment. They try to use organic methods. They use natural forms of fertilizer and no pesticides. Unfortunately, these methods do not yield as much grain.

Producing food is important. However, I am concerned about damage to the environment of the plains.

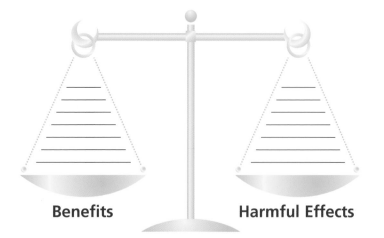

Benefits

Harmful Effects

Do ◆ Discuss ◆ Discover

1. Brainstorm as many things as you can that come from farms in the Interior Plains region.
2. What are organic methods of farming? Give one example.
3. With your class, talk about the benefits of using pesticides and fertilizers. Then talk about ways they can harm people and the environment.

Chapter 3

Knowledge and Understanding

1. Draw a physical region organizer similar to the one you did on page 27 of Chapter 2. Write the title "The Interior Plains" at the top. Use information from this chapter and your notes to fill in every area of the organizer. Put it into your notebook.

2. Identify vocabulary from this chapter to add to the vocabulary section of your notebook. Draw diagrams or sketches to help you remember the words and their meanings.

3. Look at the following four pictures. Describe what each tells you about the Interior Plains region.

Inquiry/Research and Communication Skills

4. Study the ingredients on three different cereal boxes. List the names of the cereals and the types of grain used in them.

Map, Globe, and Graphic Skills

5. Identify the major waterways on a map of the Interior Plains region. Remember to include a legend, compass rose, and colour.

Application

6. Create a postcard about the Interior Plains region. Show one or more important characteristics of this region. On the back of the postcard, explain why this image represents the Interior Plains region to you.

The Canada Project

1. Find the outline map of Canada you started at the end of Chapter 2. Colour the Interior Plains region. Label the provinces/territories that are in the Interior Plains region. Add important information about the Interior Plains region to your map. (Use the maps on page 28 and inside the front and back covers of the text to help.)

2. Find a special image, or create your own, that gives information and creates a feeling about your province/territory. On the back, describe in your own words the foreground, middle ground, and background of the image.

Chapter 4
The Arctic Lowlands

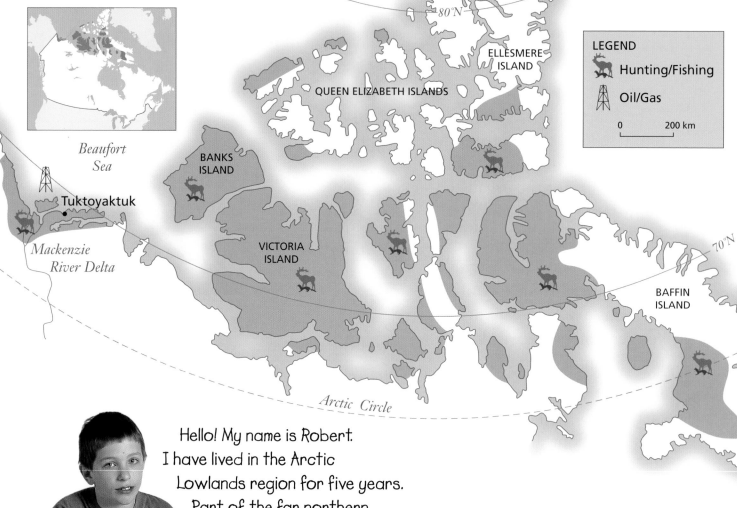

80°N

ELLESMERE ISLAND

QUEEN ELIZABETH ISLANDS

LEGEND
🦌 Hunting/Fishing
⛽ Oil/Gas
0   200 km

Beaufort Sea

BANKS ISLAND

Tuktoyaktuk

Mackenzie River Delta

VICTORIA ISLAND

70°N

BAFFIN ISLAND

Arctic Circle

Hello! My name is Robert. I have lived in the Arctic Lowlands region for five years. Part of the far northern coast of Canada and many islands in the Arctic Ocean make up this small region. It includes parts of the Yukon, the Northwest Territories, and Nunavut. It does not include the mountainous islands at the very top of Canada.

Almost all of the Arctic Lowlands region is found north of the Arctic Circle. The Arctic Circle is at 66½° N latitude.

Focus on Learning

In this chapter, you will learn about
- the physical features of the Arctic Lowlands region
- the climate of the region
- the vegetation of the region
- the animal life of the region
- the natural resources of the region
- notemaking
- identifying concerns

Vocabulary

Arctic Circle
permafrost
tundra
treeline

barren
adaptation
non-renewable resources

42

NEL

Physical Features

The Arctic Lowlands region is made up mostly of low-lying islands and parts of the northern shore of Canada. About 18 000 years ago, the temperatures on Earth were much lower. All of this land was covered by glaciers. This period was called an ice age.

In areas with permafrost, you can also see rounded hills called pingos. *Pingo* is an Inuit word for these landforms. Pingos have a core of solid ice. They gradually grow larger as more water freezes onto the ice in the centre of the hill.

These tourists are photographing a large pingo on the delta of the Mackenzie River.

The shoreline is low-lying, but some northern islands have higher elevations.

The Arctic Lowlands region has large areas of rock and boggy plains. Soils are thin and not very good for growing plants. Only the surface thaws in summer. The ground below remains frozen all year round. This is called **permafrost**.

In winter, sea ice forms in the salt water of the ocean and the passages between islands, called straits. In summer, the sea ice melts and breaks up into floating sheets of ice, called ice floes. Ice floes may be a few metres across or many kilometres across.

These Narwhal whales need to find breaks in the sea ice to come up to breathe.

These caribou can be seen from a distance because much of the land of the Arctic Lowlands region is flat.

Climate

Temperature

Summer in the Arctic Lowlands region is brief but sunny. In the middle of the summer, the Sun does not set all night long. It rarely gets hot, but summers are warm and skies are clear. It can reach 15° C on a summer day.

The winters are very cold and long. In January, temperatures can reach a low of –45° C. In the middle of the winter, the Sun does not come above the horizon at all.

Plants such as these mountain avens form seeds quickly because the summer is very brief.

Precipitation

There is little precipitation in the Arctic Lowlands region. In the summer, rainfall is not common. Some snow falls in the winter. However, this region gets less snow than most other regions of Canada.

Northern Lights brighten up the dark sky. These moving sheets of light are caused by energy from the Sun acting on particles in the air.

Houses and clothing must protect people from the extreme cold.

Hours of Sunlight

Dec. 21
0.0 hours

Mar. 21
12.5 hours

June 21
24.0 hours

Sept. 21
12.5 hours

Vegetation

The physical features and climate of the Arctic Lowlands region affect the plants that grow there. Thin soils, cold temperatures, low precipitation, a short summer, and permafrost all affect vegetation.

Only small scattered plants, mosses, and low-growing shrubs grow in the region. The name for this area of low Arctic vegetation is **tundra**. During the long summer days, many small plants produce bright flowers.

Some places are **barren**. This means they have few living plants. Tundra vegetation grows slowly. If the environment is damaged, plants will take a very long time to grow again.

Tundra is similar to the vegetation above the treeline on high mountains. That is the line past which trees can no longer grow.

This freshly caught Arctic char is lying on tundra vegetation.

Animal Life

Animals that live in the Arctic Lowlands region have made **adaptations** to help them live there. That means their bodies have special features that help them survive. Land animals have thick fur. Many have white coats or turn white in winter so they are difficult to see. Some of the land animals are caribou, muskoxen, polar bears, wolves, Arctic foxes, and Arctic hares.

The ocean waters contain marine animals. Whales, seals, and walruses are found there. They have adapted to the cold water and ice by having a thick layer of fat called blubber under their skins. They can swim under the ice. However, they must find holes in the ice or open water to come up to breathe.

Many birds live in the Arctic Lowlands region in summer. Loons, snow geese, snowy owls, and ivory gulls nest in the region. They raise their young and then migrate farther south in the autumn.

Peary caribou are found only on a few Arctic islands. They are an endangered species.

Snowy owls hunt for food in the daytime.

Do ◆ Discuss ◆ Discover

Write answers to these questions in your notebook.

1. What are two ways in which the tops of high mountains and the Arctic Lowlands region are similar?
2. Why would having a white coat in winter be an advantage for a hare and for a fox?

The Gift of the Whale

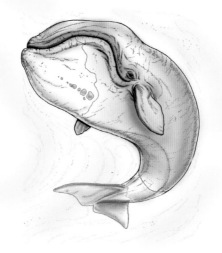

When the Great Spirit created this land, he made many beautiful and good things. He made the sun and the moon and the stars. He made the wide land, white with snow, and the mountains and the ocean. He made fish of all kinds and the many birds. He made the seals and the walrus and the great bears. Then the Great Spirit made the Inupiaq. He had a special love for the people and showed them how to live, using everything around them.

Then after making all this, the Great Spirit decided to make one thing more. This would be the best creation of all. The Great Spirit made this being with great care. It was the Bowhead Whale. It was, indeed, the most beautiful and the finest of the things made by the Great Spirit. As it swam, it flowed through the ocean. It sang as it went, and it was in perfect balance with everything around it.

But the Great Spirit saw something else. He saw that the Inupiaq people needed the Bowhead Whale. Without the whale, it would be hard for them to survive. They needed to eat *muktuk*, the flesh of the whale, to keep warm and healthy during the long, cold nights. They needed its bones to help build their homes. They needed every part of the great whale.

So the Great Spirit gave the Bowhead to the Inupiaq. He gave them a way to hunt it from their boats covered with walrus hide. He made a special time each spring, when the ice of the ocean would break apart to form a road where the whales would swim. In that whale road, the Open Lead, the whales would come to the surface and wait there to be struck by the harpoons of the Inupiaq. They would continue to do so every year as long as the Inupiaq showed respect to the Bowhead, as long as the Inupiaq only took the few whales that they needed in order to survive.

But the Great Spirit decided this also. At that time each year when the Open Lead formed, when the whales came to the surface to be hunted, the Great Spirit made it so that a heavy cloud of thick mist would hang just above the ice, just above the heads of the whales and the Inupiaq. That thick mist would hang there between the sea and the sky. "Though I give you permission to kill my most perfect creation," the Great Spirit said, "I do not wish to watch it."

— A traditional story
of the Inupiaq

Do ◆ Discuss ◆ Discover

1. Discuss with a partner why people should conserve and show respect for the world around them.

2. In your notes, explain why the Bowhead whales should be protected. Use information from the text and your own ideas to support your answer.

Horns and Paws

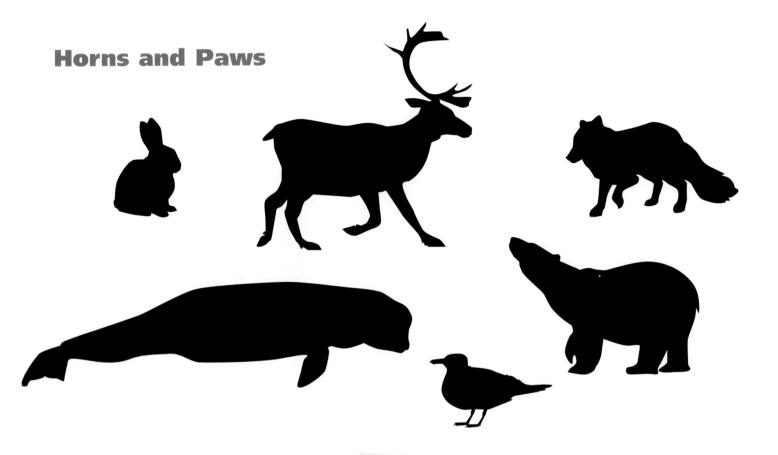

Arctic Lowlands Arts

My North

Sharing a Story
Unique
Built by many hands
Symbol of the Arctic.
Pile of rocks
Slabs and stones
A figure?
Showing the way home
Warning of danger
Directing to food
Celebrating an event
Pointing to a stationary star
More than a marker
Symbol of strength
My North
My Arctic.

Inuksuks are easily seen on the landscape of the North.

Do ◆ Discuss ◆ Discover

Do the following questions in groups of three.

1. Use a variety of sources (books, Internet, encyclopedia) to help you name the animals represented by the six shadow figures above.

2. Discuss what you know about the animals in the Arctic Lowlands region.

3. Use an organizer (see page 12) to compare them with what you have learned about animals in other parts of Canada. Put this into your notebook.

The Earth and the People

The earth was here before
   the people.
The very first people
Came out of the ground.
Everything came from the
   ground,
Even caribou.
Children once grew
Out of the ground
Just as flowers do.
Women out wandering
   found them sprawling on
   the grass
And took them home and
   nursed them.
That way people multiplied.
This land of ours
Has become habitable
Because we came here
And learned how to hunt.

       — Traditional Inuit song

Bessie Hikomak and Martina Anavilok with Bessie's sealskin tapestry

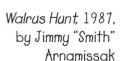

Walrus Hunt, 1987, by Jimmy "Smith" Arnamissak

Do ◆ Discuss ◆ Discover

1. In your small group, discuss the things the songwriter says about the earth. Share your group's thoughts with the rest of the class. Then answer this question in your notebook:

   a) How does the songwriter guide you to understand that the earth was the source of life?

2. Discuss how the sculpture and tapestry represent life in the Arctic Lowlands region.

3. Draw a picture showing your favourite part of this song or create a design for a sculpture or tapestry that represents the Arctic Lowlands region. (This could go into your project scrapbook or shoebox, or into your notebook.)

Arctic Life – Then and Now

There are many ways in which technology has changed the lives of people living in communities in the Arctic Lowlands region. Look at the two sets of photographs on this page. One could have taken place during Robert's great-grandfather's days; the other is of today.

THEN

NOW

Do ◆ Discuss ◆ Discover

1. Look at the photographs. Describe in your notebook how technology has changed the way of life of the people in this region. Use the information from the text and your own ideas to support your answers.

Natural Resources

The Arctic Lowlands region has few renewable resources other than its animal life. There is no farmland or forest. The animals and sea life provide important food and clothing resources for the people who live there. Some products are sold outside the region.

The region has important **non-renewable resources** such as zinc, lead, oil, natural gas, and coal. These are called non-renewable because they disappear after being used.

These oil-drilling ships with towers are frozen in the pack ice on the Beaufort Sea.

Diamonds, gold, and sapphires are found on Baffin Island in Nunavut.

A large oil field lies below the Beaufort Sea and the Mackenzie Delta of the Northwest Territories. Oil companies have been exploring and drilling test wells in the Mackenzie Delta and offshore in the Beaufort Sea since the 1970s.

The cost of producing and transporting oil and gas to markets farther south is very high. There is still no large production of oil and gas in this part of the region.

Some products from the region, besides minerals, are sold elsewhere in Canada and the world. These include furs, frozen fish such as Arctic char, and works of art such as soapstone sculptures.

The Arctic char is similar to the salmon. These fish are a source of food and income for people in the region.

Soapstone is an easily carved rock found in many places in Canada, including the far North. Inuit artists have created soapstone sculptures that have been sold around the world.

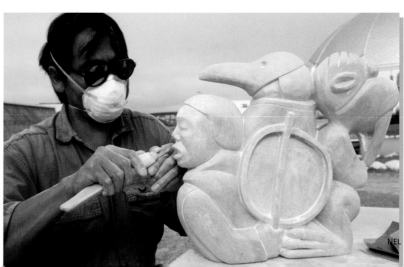

Inuit sculptures usually show the relationship between the people and the animals of the region.

Notemaking

Your notebook is a place to keep information about what you have studied in class. You may also include notes made when doing research or reading for information. Making notes will help you remember. You can use your notes to study for tests or prepare for projects. Notes can be in different forms, such as

- point-form notes (main topics and related details)
- notes in a chart or organizer
- notes in a web (to show connections between ideas)
- pictures, diagrams, timelines

Organizing Your Notes

1. Put the date at the top of each new set of notes.

2. Give each day's work a title. If you used the textbook, write the page number with your notes.

3. Underline the title and the date with a coloured pencil and ruler.

4. Make brief notes but include all of the important topics and some important details about the topics.

Writing Point-Form Notes

1. Point-form notes don't need to be sentences, just key phrases.

2. Reread the passage. Use the main idea as a title.

3. List the topic of each paragraph. These are the main ideas of the passage.

4. Under each topic, list key words and supporting details from the paragraph.

5. You may want to draw pictures beside each topic to remind you.

6. Underline or highlight key words and definitions.

Example

Natural Resources (Arctic Lowlands region)
- renewable resources
    - few renewable resources
    - no farmland or forests
    - animal and sea life
- non-renewable resources
    - zinc, lead, oil, natural gas, coal
    - <u>non-renewable means they disappear after being used</u>
- minerals and oil
    - lead and zinc
    - oil exploration
- other products
    - furs, fish, soapstone art

Arctic Oil and Gas Exploration

Oil and gas fields are found under both the land and the oceans of the world. Drilling for oil and gas in the Arctic Lowlands region presents many challenges. Some challenges are sea ice, the storms, the cold, the remote location, and the sensitive environment.

Several kinds of offshore drilling rigs have been developed. Some platforms float. Some are built on long pillars or artificial islands. Drill ships with very strong hulls have been used in some deep-water areas.

The environment of the Mackenzie River Delta is fragile and easily damaged. Heat from buildings, machinery, and people raise the temperature of the ground. When the permafrost begins to melt underneath, the ground turns into bog. Equipment and buildings can sink below the surface.

Most Arctic exploration is done far away from populated places. Welders, mechanics, electricians, engineers, and drilling specialists

Exploration wells are drilled to locate sources of oil and gas.

stay at a well site for long periods. Cooks, firefighters, computer technicians, and helicopter pilots also live on the site. It is like working on a ship far from shore.

Oil and gas workers earn extra money for working in harsh conditions.

Even though the companies make sure they work carefully, oil spills are possible. It is very difficult to clean up a spill in such a severe climate. The people in the area hope the oil companies will never have to test their disaster plans.

People and supplies are transported by air.

Do ◆ Discuss ◆ Discover

1. In your notebook, write point-form notes about this information on Arctic oil and gas exploration.

2. Look back at page 51. Review the list of different ways to make notes. What kinds of information about Arctic oil and gas exploration would you record on a web or chart? Share your ideas with one other student and then complete either a web or a chart to put into your notebook.

Pen Pals

From: **Amorak** | Subject: **Pen pal** | To: **John Paul** | Date: **November 24**

Hello, John Paul.

My name is Amorak. It means Spirit of the Wolf. I am 9 years old and I live near Tuktoyaktuk. I was very excited to hear about this pen pal project. I think it will be great to be able to share what my life is like with someone who lives in a different place.

I get ready for school each morning by turning on the television. My teacher, Ms. Pokiak, teaches all her students using satellite television because most of us are too far from a school. I do my homework on the computer and e-mail it to her. When she is done looking at it, she sends it back to me. I think going to school at home is cool.

When I finish my school work, I like to play outside with my friends. I also like to play computer games and read stories about superheroes and brave children.

I help out around the house by getting dinner started. I love fresh vegetables, especially lettuce and tomatoes. During winter, we don't always get them, so we usually eat canned vegetables at dinner. When the supply plane comes in, we go to meet it on our snowmobiles so we can get fresh food and mail. This is an exciting time for me! I hope I hear from you soon.

Your friend,
Amorak

From: **John Paul** | Subject: **Pen pal** | To: **Amorak** | Date: **November 25**

Hello, Amorak.

My name is John Paul. I have two names because my parents wanted me to remember both of my grandfathers. My parents and teachers call me by both names, but all my friends call me JP.
I am 10 years old. I live in Mississauga.

At school, we go outside to play at recess in the morning for 15 minutes and in the afternoon, too. At lunchtime, we go outside for 45 minutes unless it is really cold. When the temperature reaches −15° C, the principal tells us to stay in because it is too cold. My teacher, Mrs. Haley, always has interesting things to do. She lets us pick the books we want to read and we talk about them. She does not give us too much homework. After school, I go home on the school bus.

When it is warm outside, I play road hockey and soccer with my friends. I also like to watch television or listen to music. What is your favourite music? I love playing computer games, too. Maybe we could play a game online together.

My parents both drive to work. My mom is a nurse in a doctor's office, and my dad manages a hotel. They work hard, so when they come home, I try to help if I can.

Here is a picture of me getting on the school bus.

Talk to you soon,
John Paul

Robert's Concern

My family and I live in Tuktoyaktuk, Northwest Territories. My father works for a company that drills for oil. Many people want the oil company here because the company promised us new roads, more business, and a better airport.

and disturbs the permafrost. This creates deep boggy places.

When plants in this environment die, it is a very long time before others grow. If the land or ocean is polluted, many animals, birds, and fish die. Some kinds, like muskoxen, are found only in the Arctic. If their habitat changes, they will be endangered.

People who live here depend on the environment for food. As the community changes and the population increases, there are more needs to be met. More food and products are imported. More energy is used to heat buildings and run machinery. More waste and garbage are produced. Garbage cannot be buried because of the permafrost. It is a hazard for the birds and wildlife of the region.

Travel on the tundra creates deep ruts in summer. It kills plants

I am concerned that the changes in the community will cause permanent changes in the environment. We need to think about how to prevent this.

Do ◆ Discuss ◆ Discover

1. Discuss why plants grow so slowly in this region. Review the Physical Features, Climate, and Vegetation sections in this chapter.
2. What three things about the environment would you tell people new to the Arctic Lowlands region to help protect it?

Chapter 4

Knowledge and Understanding

1. Draw a region organizer similar to the one you did on page 41 of Chapter 3. Write the title "The Arctic Lowlands" at the top. Use information from this chapter and your notes to fill in every area of the organizer. Put it into your notebook.

2. Identify vocabulary from this chapter to add to the vocabulary section of your notebook. Draw diagrams or sketches to help you remember the words and their meanings.

3. Explain in a paragraph how animals have adapted to the climate of the Arctic Lowlands region.

Inquiry/Research and Communication Skills

4. Research the muskox. Follow the research model on page 14. Choose a form of notemaking and write notes about the muskox. (This could go into your scrapbook or shoebox.)

Map, Globe, and Graphic Skills

5. On an outline of a globe, draw and label the Arctic Circle (66½° N latitude). Create your own pictorial symbols to show the hours of daylight in all four seasons at the Arctic Circle.

Application

6. Describe in two paragraphs how your daily schedule might change if it were daylight for 23 hours a day where you live.

7. Using the information from the e-mails on page 53, complete a comparison chart (see page 12) to describe the lives of the two pen pals. Remember that a comparison chart needs a list of criteria.

The Canada Project

1. Find the outline map of Canada you started at the end of Chapter 2. Colour the Arctic Lowlands region. Label the provinces/territories that are in the Arctic Lowlands region. Add important information about the Arctic Lowlands region to your map. (Use the maps on page 42 and inside the front and back covers of the text to help.)

2. Create a sculpture or locate a small figurine of one animal that lives in your province/territory to put into your shoebox.

3. Research a legend, poem, or song from your province/territory to put into your scrapbook or shoebox. Add your own illustrations to make it interesting and fun.

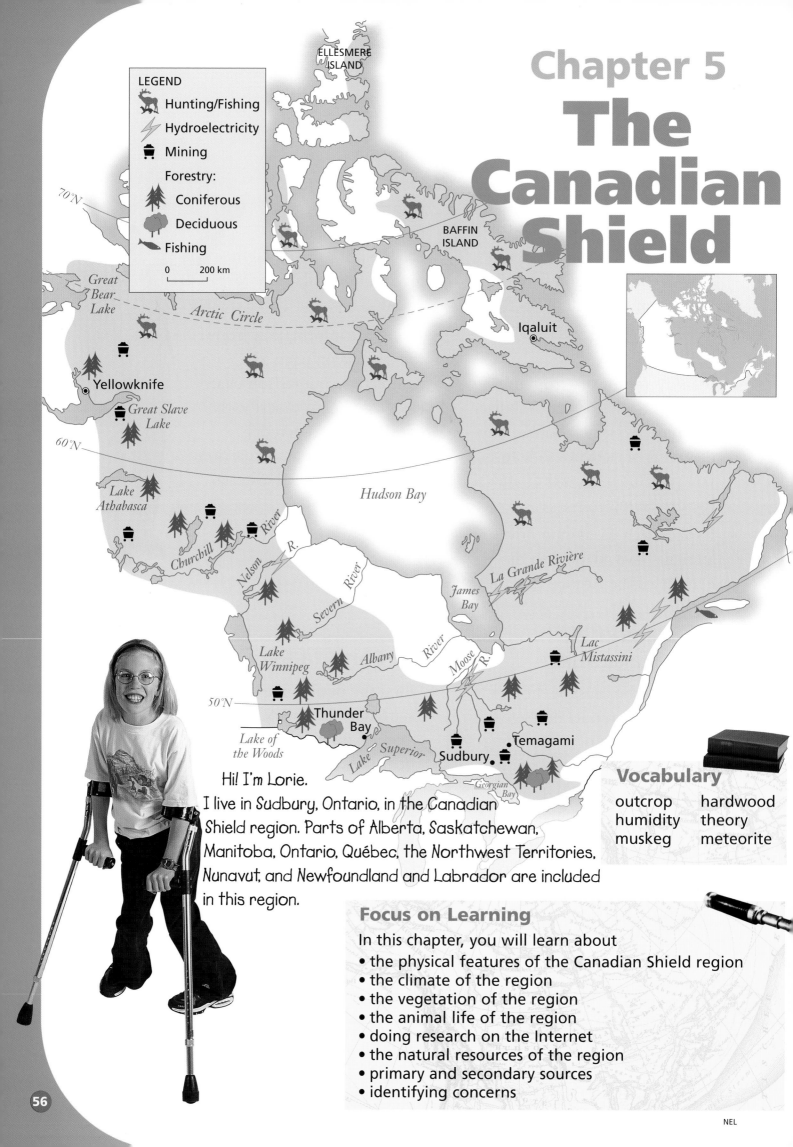

Chapter 5
The Canadian Shield

LEGEND

- Hunting/Fishing
- Hydroelectricity
- Mining
- Forestry:
  - Coniferous
  - Deciduous
- Fishing

0   200 km

ELLESMERE ISLAND

BAFFIN ISLAND

70°N

Great Bear Lake

Arctic Circle

Iqaluit

Yellowknife

Great Slave Lake

60°N

Lake Athabasca

Hudson Bay

Churchill

Nelson River

R.

Severn River

Albany

River

James Bay

Moose R.

La Grande Rivière

Lac Mistassini

Lake Winnipeg

50°N

Thunder Bay

Lake of the Woods

Lake Superior

Sudbury

Temagami

Georgian Bay

Hi! I'm Lorie.
I live in Sudbury, Ontario, in the Canadian Shield region. Parts of Alberta, Saskatchewan, Manitoba, Ontario, Québec, the Northwest Territories, Nunavut, and Newfoundland and Labrador are included in this region.

Vocabulary

outcrop   hardwood
humidity   theory
muskeg   meteorite

Focus on Learning

In this chapter, you will learn about
- the physical features of the Canadian Shield region
- the climate of the region
- the vegetation of the region
- the animal life of the region
- doing research on the Internet
- the natural resources of the region
- primary and secondary sources
- identifying concerns

Physical Features

The Canadian Shield region covers about half of Canada. The landforms are similar everywhere in the region. It has rocky hills and thousands of lakes, rivers, streams, and marshes. The layer of soil over rock is thin in most places. Many **outcrops** of bare rock show through it.

The glaciers of the ice age spread across this region. The weight of the ice scraped the surface of the rocky hills. In many places, you can see long scratches on the rock. These were made when stones frozen in the ice of a glacier dragged across the bedrock.

First Snow, North Shore of Lake Superior by Lawren S. Harris

Loose rock and soil were pushed and dragged great distances. When the glaciers melted and retreated, the rock and soil were left behind, creating hills and gravel beds.

Many river systems of the Canadian Shield region flow towards Hudson Bay. Other rivers flow into the Great Lakes and St. Lawrence River system, which flows to the Atlantic Ocean.

Rocky outcrops are typical of the Canadian Shield region.

Do ◆ Discuss ◆ Discover

1. With a partner, carefully examine the painting *First Snow, North Shore of Lake Superior* by Lawren S. Harris.
   a) What do you see in the foreground, middle ground, and background?
   b) What seems to be the most important thing in the painting?
   c) What natural thing do you think scratched the rocks? How?
   d) What season do you associate with these colours?
   e) What do you think this painting says about what this region is like? Use the information from the text and your own ideas to support your answers.
2. On your own, imitate the style of the painting. Paint a picture of your neighbourhood during the same season. Put this into your notebook.

Hands On!

This experiment will show you how a glacier moves and changes the land.

You will need

- a 20 x 30 x 10 cm cake pan
- water
- a handful of very cold pebbles
- 1 cm of sand in a large flat baking tray (or use a sand table)

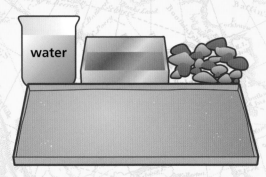

1. Put 5 cm of water in the cake pan and freeze it. Put the pebbles in the freezer to get cold.

2. Remove the sheet of ice from the cake pan. Place the cold pebbles on top of the sand in the tray and place the sheet of ice on top. Press down on the ice, the pebbles, and the sand. Let the ice sit for a while. Notice that sand and pebbles have attached to the bottom of the ice, making the bottom surface bumpy and sandy.

3. Slide the ice sheet slowly along the sand. Notice that a mound of sand is pushed ahead of the ice sheet. Notice the trench that the ice sheet carves as it moves. Notice the grooves that the pebbles scratch on the sandy surface. Push the ice sheet from one end of the tray of sand to the other.

4. Leave the ice sitting on the sand to melt.

5. Every half hour, observe the progress of the melting ice. As the ice melts, observe that the material pushed by the ice sheet is left behind. It marks the glacier's farthest point of advance. Observe that the pebbles dragged underneath the ice sheet are deposited along the way.

6. Record your observations in writing and a diagram and put them into your notebook.

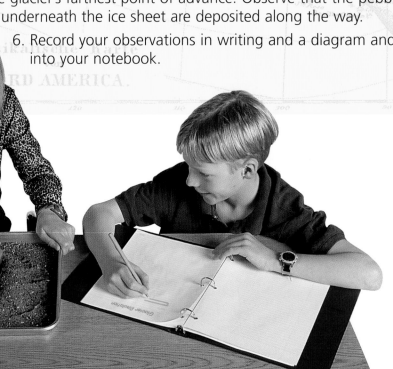

Climate

Winters in the Canadian Shield region are cold. In the far north, there is less snow. In the southern part, snowfall can be very heavy.

A winter day in the northern Canadian Shield region

A foggy day near the shore of Lake Superior

Summers in the far north are similar to the Arctic Lowlands region. They are brief, but the days are very long. Farther south, the summer is warmer and more humid. **Humidity** is the amount of water vapour in the air. The southern areas of the Canadian Shield region get up to 1600 millimetres of precipitation each year. Much of it falls as snow, but rain in the summer is also common.

Vegetation

The northern part of the area has tundra vegetation. There are small plants, mosses, and low-growing shrubs. Rocky areas are barren. Farther south, scattered coniferous trees and shrubs grow. In places where there is more soil, there are forests of coniferous trees.

Between the rocky hills are boggy wetlands called **muskeg**. Muskeg is formed as living and dead vegetation gradually fills in lakes.

Muskeg, with coniferous trees

The forests that grow farthest south in the region are mixed deciduous and coniferous trees.

In autumn, the deciduous trees turn yellow or red and the coniferous trees remain dark green.

Acid Rain

Many trees are killed by acid rain. Acid rain is formed when pollution in the air mixes with rain. This harmful rain slowly destroys things on which it falls. For example, sugar maple is a valuable tree grown in parts of this region. Mature sugar maple woods are being killed by acid rain. They will only regrow if there is no more acid rain. New trees will need many years to mature.

Animal Life

Many types of animals live in the Canadian Shield region. Some examples are woodland caribou, wolves, and foxes. In the forests, moose and deer are common.

Many fur-bearing animals make their homes in this region. Black bears, beavers, pine martens, minks, foxes, lynx, and muskrats are some examples. They grow heavy warm coats as an adaptation to the winter cold.

Freshwater fish are plentiful in the lakes and rivers. Lake trout, bass, perch, pickerel, and whitefish are common freshwater fish. Fish grow very large because there is little commercial fishing. Fly-in sport fishing is an industry that takes advantage of the unspoiled environment and plentiful fish.

Doing Research on the Internet

The Internet is a powerful research tool. Do Internet research work at school with the guidance of your teacher or at home with your parents. To research on the Internet, you need to learn how to properly use a search engine.

1. Get on the Internet.

2. Locate the search engine. Two common ones are Yahoo! Kids and Google. Usually, your Internet menu bar will have a button called "Search."

3. You need to define your search. Type key words to direct the search engine. For example: Ontario, Canada.

4. Notice the number of entries. You need to narrow the search.

5. Choose a more specific entry. For example, begin a new search for a place in Ontario, such as a town or city.

6. Notice the number of entries. There should be fewer.

7. Read the entries to find one that you think will be useful. Notice the web address. If it ends with .ca, it is an address in Canada. If it ends with .on.ca, it is an address in Ontario.

8. Be sure to keep a record of where you find information on the Internet. Write the web address in your notes and add the date you visited it.

Natural Resources

The Canadian Shield is a region rich with natural resources. Both softwood and **hardwood** are harvested from the forests. Softwood from coniferous forests is used for pulp, paper, and lumber for construction. Hardwood is used for building furniture, cabinets, and wall panelling. Maple, oak, birch, and walnut are all valued for their beautiful, strong wood.

Many rivers in the region are used to make hydroelectricity. Some hydroelectric power is sold to other regions.

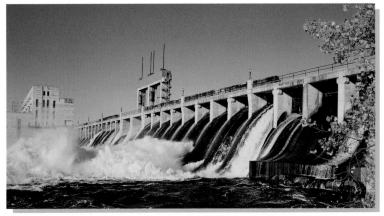

A hydroelectric power plant at Seven Sisters Falls on the Winnipeg River produces electricity used in the Interior Plains region.

Sawmills cut trees into lumber for construction materials.

Mining is one of the most important industries in this region. Minerals found in the Canadian Shield region include copper, iron, lead, nickel, gold, silver, uranium, and zinc. Because of the resources in this region, Canada is now one of the world's top three diamond producers.

Mine workers need to be strong and willing to work underground in uncomfortable conditions.

Some mines are underground. Others, such as this one, are surface mines, sometimes called open-pit mines.

Do ◆ Discuss ◆ Discover

1. Use the guideline on the previous page to plan an Internet search for information about one resource of the Canadian Shield region that is found in Ontario. What key words would you use? How would you narrow the search if you did not find something suitable the first time?

Wind Farms

This wind farm produces electricity for homes and businesses.

Believe it or not, you can farm the wind. In fact, wind farms are cropping up all over Canada. Unlike other farms, however, wind farms do not produce food. Instead, they produce energy.

Wind power uses the wind to generate electricity. Wind energy is the fastest-growing source of electricity in the world.

A wind turbine usually has two or three large blades, like those on a propeller airplane. These strong but light blades are attached to machinery on the top of a tall tower.

Wind turbines create electrical energy by turning a generator.

Many wind turbines used together form a wind farm that makes electricity to power homes and businesses.

Wind energy is clean, so it does not produce any air pollution. It is less harmful to the environment than some other sources of energy. Wind energy is also a renewable resource.

There are wind farms all across Canada. They can generate enough electricity for over 400 000 homes.

The largest wind farm in Canada is found in Ontario.

How It Works

1 The tower holds the blades up high where strong winds blow.

2 The wind turns the blades.

3 The blades spin the rotor.

4 The rotor turns the gears.

5 The gears turn a generator that makes electricity.

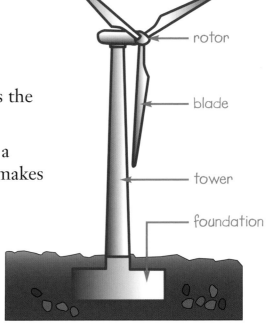

rotor

blade

tower

foundation

Do ◆ Discuss ◆ Discover

1. In a small group, discuss the possible benefits and disadvantages to using wind as a renewable source of power.

2. Record your group's discussion points on chart paper. Present them to the class.

Temagami – A Forestry Community

Temagami is a township in Ontario with fewer than 1000 people. It is 100 kilometres north of North Bay. The name of the township is pronounced "te-MAWG-a-mee." It is an Ojibway word meaning "deep water by the shore." The township is surrounded by pine forests, clear waters, and bountiful fish and wildlife.

Temagami has been known for outdoor and wilderness recreation for over 100 years. Cottages, fishing and hunting lodges, and hotels dot the area. One-third of the last surviving ancient white and red pine forest in the world is found around Temagami. There are 25 kilometres of trails through old uncut forests.

The Temagami area was first logged in the 1920s and 1930s. There are interesting places for visitors to learn about the early lumbering industry. Old camps, sawmills, log chutes, and fire towers can be visited.

There is a historic fire tower on a hill above Temagami. Forest rangers watched from the tower for forest fires. If danger was spotted, they directed fire crews to the location. The fire tower is now a site for tourists to visit.

Temagami is set amidst the lakes and trees of the Canadian Shield region.

Trails and boardwalks through wetlands allow visitors to see the environment up close.

The fire tower on the hill is a local landmark.

Visit Temagami

1. a) Do an Internet search for Temagami, Ontario, to find out more about the community.

   b) Go to www.duvaleducation.com/ourcountry canada2. Click on the link to the Temagami Fire Tower to take a visual tour of the area around the fire tower.

Do ◆ Discuss ◆ Discover

1. Imagine you are a forest ranger. Write a letter to your family or a friend about what being a forest ranger might be like.

Minerals of Ontario

The Canadian Shield region covers two-thirds of Ontario. Mining has been important to Ontario since the early 1800s. Ontario's first gold rush took place near the town of Madoc in 1866.

Today, Ontario is one of the world's top 10 mineral producers. It produces more than 30 different minerals. Eighty per cent of Ontario's mineral production is sold around the world.

Nickel, gold, copper, uranium, zinc, platinum, cobalt, and silver are examples of minerals mined in Ontario. Many towns in northern Ontario were built because of mining activities. Metals such as steel are manufactured from a combination of minerals.

Amethyst is the official mineral of the province of Ontario. This piece was found near Thunder Bay.

A Theory About Minerals

Scientists have developed **theories** about why this area is so rich in minerals. Theories are ideas that people think could be true because there is a lot of evidence to support them, but they have not been proven.

One theory is that some of the minerals came from **meteorites**. Meteorites are rocks from outer space that crash into the Earth. Scientists think the meteorites may have contained minerals that are now being mined. The impact of a meteorite would form a huge circular hollow, like the craters on the surface of the Moon. The mineral ores would melt in the impact and then cool.

Do ◆ Discuss ◆ Discover

Choose one of the following two activities to complete with a partner.

1. a) Locate and then place these mining towns and cities on a map of Ontario: Red Lake, Hemlo, Wawa, Elliot Lake, Timmins, Manitouwadge, Sudbury, and Kirkland Lake.

   b) Research the minerals mined near these towns and cities.

   c) Decide which symbols you could use to represent the minerals mined in these locations.

   d) Create a legend of symbols for your map and add the symbols beside the locations on your map.

2. a) Research two theories of why the Sudbury area is so rich in minerals. If you use the Internet, begin your search using these key words:
   • meteorite, Sudbury Basin
   • magma, Sudbury Basin

   b) Decide which theory is more interesting to you. Explain your reasons in a paragraph and put it into your notebook.

Minerals and Metals in Our Lives

Take a walk around your home and look at the items you use each day. Minerals and metals are often part of what is used to make these items. Think about which minerals and metals were used to create the items you see. Use this web to help you identify them.

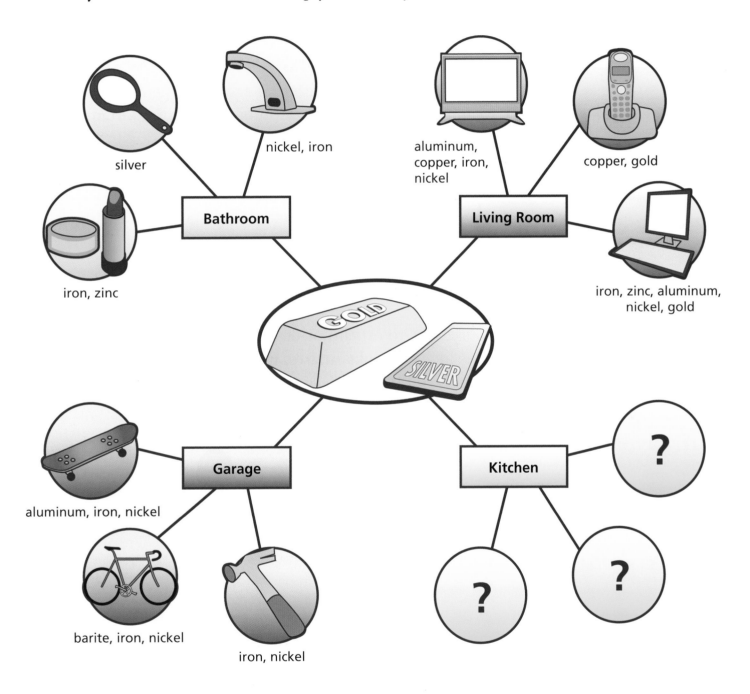

Do ◆ Discuss ◆ Discover

1. Think about the items containing minerals and metals you found in your kitchen. List them in your notebook.
2. With a partner, discuss the kinds of minerals and metals that may have been used to make the items.
3. Complete the kitchen part of the web in your notebook.

Primary and Secondary Sources

Primary Sources

Primary sources are accurate records of events told by people who were there. Items such as letters, diary entries, interviews, or photographs are considered primary sources. Data is also considered a primary source.

Gather some data by surveying some people you know:

1. Find five people of different ages. Ask them which four minerals and metals they think are most important in their lives. Have each person write down the minerals and metals in order from most important to least important.

2. Collect the sheets and make a tally chart of their choices.

3. Write a statement summarizing the results of your tally chart.

Secondary Sources

Secondary sources try to explain or describe a primary event. Secondary sources include books, atlases, magazines, or articles on the Internet. The writers of the secondary sources draw conclusions about primary source information.

1. Research the top three minerals and metals used in manufacturing that are mined or produced in Canada. Use the Internet and your teacher's guidance to do your research.

2. Choose one room in your home. Make a list of the minerals and metals you see in this room.

3. Based on your research and what you know, write a statement about the minerals and metals you have decided are the most important.

Do ◆ Discuss ◆ Discover

1. Compare the results of the primary source survey with your secondary source research. Write two summary statements.

Sudbury – A Mining Community

The city of Sudbury sits in a huge oval-shaped dent in the rocky Canadian Shield region. This basin is 60 kilometres by 27 kilometres. It holds one of the Earth's richest-known deposits of nickel and copper. Mining is a $3-billion-a-year business for Sudbury. One of the world's largest deposits of nickel is found there.

Sudbury is the largest city in northeastern Ontario.

Industries brought wealth but created problems for the region. Soils became polluted and topsoil was eroded. Blackened bare rock outcrops with scattered, unhealthy plants surrounded Sudbury. Many people said it looked like the surface of the Moon!

The people of Sudbury have worked with the mining industry to bring the region back to life. Over the past two decades, people have planted more than 5 million trees. Today, weather records show that air pollution levels in Sudbury are lower than in Toronto or Hamilton. The United Nations recently honoured the Region of Sudbury for its land-recovery program.

The Big Nickel is a replica of a Canadian five cent piece, 9 metres high and 61 centimetres thick!

Mining and the processing of minerals have created many jobs for people. Sudbury is a centre of government, business, education, health care, and services.

Guided tours take you deep below the Earth's surface.

Visit Sudbury

1. If you can visit Sudbury, visit the home of the Big Nickel. You can take an underground tour and learn how mining methods have changed over the past century. Find out how it feels to be a real miner!

Do ◆ Discuss ◆ Discover

1. Write an imaginary postcard from Sudbury to put in the only underground mailbox in Canada. Draw your own picture on the front and write a message to a friend on the back.

Lorie's Concern

My father works with the regional Conservation Authority. He says that Sudbury looks much better than it used to.

For a long time, we did not pay attention to how the land around us was affected. Then people began to notice that there weren't very many plants around and that very few fish lived in the lake. The area looked bad. Trees had died, and other vegetation looked sick.

My father and the people who lived here made sure that the mining companies started to pay attention. Soon they were building taller smokestacks to carry away the smoke. Efforts were made to clean the water and the soil. People worked together to replant grasses, shrubs, and trees.

We are proud of our city. However, we are concerned that the same mistakes not be made in the future. We must not forget about what the environment needs to be healthy.

IN THE PAST

PRESENT DAY

Do ◆ Discuss ◆ Discover

1. Look at the pictures on this page. Discuss the differences you see.

2. Discuss what ideas you get from the photos that demonstrate what people can do to improve their environment.

Chapter 5

Knowledge and Understanding

1. Draw a region organizer similar to the one you did on page 55 of Chapter 4. Write the title "The Canadian Shield" at the top. Use information from this chapter and your notes to fill in every area of the organizer. Put it into your notebook.

2. Identify vocabulary from this chapter to add to the vocabulary section of your notebook. Draw diagrams or sketches to help you remember the words and their meanings.

3. Using the map legend on page 56, create an organizer listing the natural resources of the Canadian Shield region and name a product made from each resource.

Inquiry/Research and Communication Skills

4. Research how acid rain affects the water cycle. Follow the research model on page 14. Go to www.duvaleducation. com/ourcountrycanada2. Click on the link to Acid Rain to learn more about acid rain. In your notebook, draw a diagram of the water cycle. In your own words, describe the harmful effects of acid rain.

Map, Globe, and Graphic Skills

5. On an outline map of the Canadian Shield region, label the different forests found in this region. Include all the necessary parts of a map.

Application

6. On the weekend, go for a walk with your family to a local park or conservation area. Find an interesting rock. Identify the type of rock. Give it a name and create a history for it. Design a background with the perfect scenery for your rock.

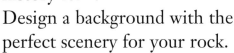

Internet Connection

7. Go to www.duvaleducation. com/ourcountrycanada2. Click on the link to Natural Resources. Read each section and create a list of products and jobs the mining industry provides for Canadian people.

The Canada Project

1. Find the outline map of Canada you started at the end of Chapter 2. Colour the Canadian Shield region. Label the provinces/territories that are in the Canadian Shield region. Add important information about the Canadian Shield region to your map. (Use the maps on page 56 and inside the front and back covers of the text to help.)

2. Create a collage of minerals found in your province/territory. Label each mineral. Try to locate actual samples of the minerals. Put your collage into your scrapbook or shoebox.

The Hudson Bay Lowlands

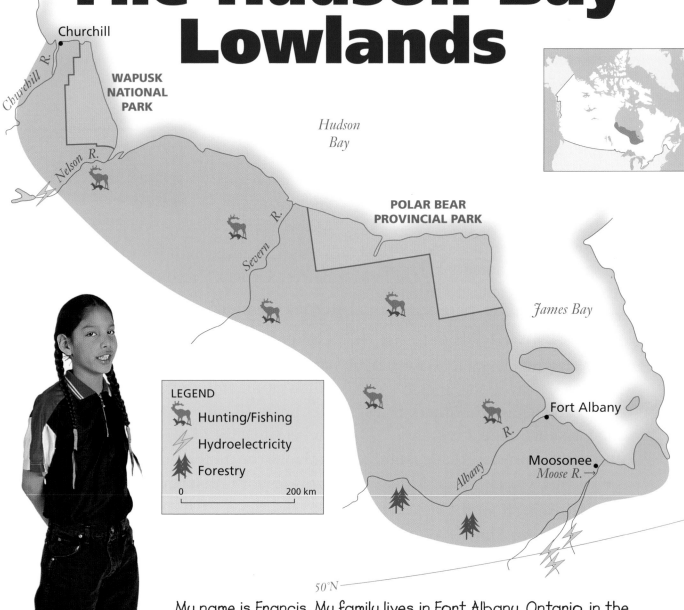

Churchill

Churchill R.

WAPUSK NATIONAL PARK

Nelson R.

Hudson Bay

Severn R.

POLAR BEAR PROVINCIAL PARK

James Bay

R.

Fort Albany

Albany R.

Moosonee
Moose R. →

LEGEND

🦌 Hunting/Fishing

⚡ Hydroelectricity

🌲 Forestry

0   200 km

50°N

My name is Francis. My family lives in Fort Albany, Ontario, in the region called the Hudson Bay Lowlands. The Hudson Bay Lowlands region stretches around the southern part of Hudson Bay and James Bay. It includes parts of Manitoba, northern Ontario, and Québec.

Focus on Learning

In this chapter, you will learn about

- the physical features of the Hudson Bay Lowlands region
- the climate of the region
- the vegetation of the region
- the animal life of the region
- the natural resources of the region
- identifying concerns

Vocabulary

peat
conservation

breed
ecotourism

Physical Features

This region is a large plain with a long coastline. It is one of the flattest parts of Canada. Once it was part of Hudson Bay. As the huge ice age glaciers retreated, the level of the land rose. This flat land was exposed and began to dry. However, it is so near to sea level that it is marshy, and water does not drain away.

Many rivers flow through the lowlands into Hudson Bay and James Bay. When the snow is melting on the Canadian Shield and Interior Plains regions, this low-lying area floods. Lands that are marshy or flooded most of the time are called wetlands.

Much of the region has permafrost. The surface of the land melts in summer and vegetation grows, but the ground remains frozen underneath. The permafrost is another reason why water does not drain away easily.

James Bay and Hudson Bay are the largest bodies of water in the world that freeze each winter and become ice-free in the summer.

The Hudson Bay Lowlands region is the world's largest wetland area, covering approximately 300 000 square kilometres.

The Hudson Bay Lowlands region is very flat. The scattered rocks here were dropped by a melting glacier.

Large chunks of ice float along the shore of Hudson Bay.

Climate

The Hudson Bay Lowlands region has long, cold winters and short, warm summers.

This region has long, cold winters.

Precipitation is moderate. Most of it falls as snow in winter. The climate is very similar to that of the northern part of the Canadian Shield region.

Tundra vegetation blooms brightly during the short summer.

The vegetation in the southwestern part of the region is more like the Canadian Shield region, with coniferous trees and muskeg.

Vegetation

The coastline of Hudson Bay and James Bay contains long marshes. Reeds and grasses of various kinds grow there.

Reeds and other wetland plants grow near the shore.

The northern part of the region is most like tundra. South of the treeline, there are scattered coniferous trees and some types of deciduous trees. Dense forests of white spruce, balsam fir, aspen and balsam poplar, and white birch grow in the southwestern part of this region.

Black spruce and tamarack grow in the muskeg. Up to 85% of the region is muskeg or peat-forming wetland. **Peat** is a deep layer of decaying plant life formed in wet conditions. It is not soil because it contains little sand or other minerals.

Do ◆ Discuss ◆ Discover

1. a) Look at the map inside the front cover of the book. Estimate the latitudes of the part of the region farthest north and the part farthest south.

   b) Discuss how these differences in latitude likely affect the climate and the vegetation.

The Wetlands – An Endangered Habitat

The Hudson Bay Lowlands region, known as the Great Muskeg, is the third-largest wetland in the world. Wetlands are nature's sponges; they store and purify water and help to maintain the water table.

The potential threats to this area are climate change, hydroelectric development, mining, and peat and petroleum extraction.

Hydroelectric development affects the duration of the ice cover and the habitats of marine mammals, fish, and birds. It also affects the water currents in and out of Hudson Bay.

Peat moss can be used as a substitute for coal as a fuel. It is also the main ingredient in potting soil. An ordinary extractor removes 22 centimetres of peat per year, but it will take 220 years to regrow this resource.

Wetlands surrounding Hudson Bay

Wetlands are the only ecosystem designated for **conservation** because they supply food and essential habitats for many species. Conservation means taking care of the environment. Wetlands provide products for food, energy, and building material. They are also valuable recreational areas for fishers, hunters, and hikers.

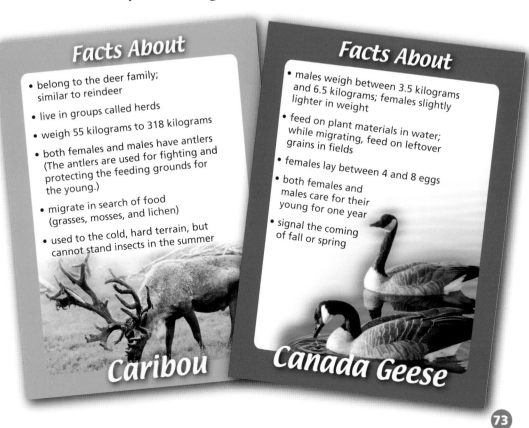

Facts About

- belong to the deer family; similar to reindeer
- live in groups called herds
- weigh 55 kilograms to 318 kilograms
- both females and males have antlers (The antlers are used for fighting and protecting the feeding grounds for the young.)
- migrate in search of food (grasses, mosses, and lichen)
- used to the cold, hard terrain, but cannot stand insects in the summer

Caribou

Facts About

- males weigh between 3.5 kilograms and 6.5 kilograms; females slightly lighter in weight
- feed on plant materials in water; while migrating, feed on leftover grains in fields
- females lay between 4 and 8 eggs
- both females and males care for their young for one year
- signal the coming of fall or spring

Canada Geese

Animal Life

Many kinds of fish, birds, and animals live and **breed** in the Hudson Bay Lowlands region. Birds lay and hatch eggs. Animals give birth and raise their young in the wetlands and forests.

Some of Canada's largest groups of snow geese and Canada geese nest along the coast. Brant geese, whistling swans, eider and merganser ducks, loons, northern phalarope, and many kinds of shorebirds also nest in the Hudson Bay Lowlands region.

Huge flocks of Canada geese live in the wetlands through the summer.

Caribou are found along the coastline in summer. They move inland among the forests in the winter. Many other Arctic mammals live there, such as Arctic foxes, lemmings, the short-tailed weasel, and Arctic hares. This region also has a large seal and walrus population.

Polar bears spend most of the winter on the sea. They mainly eat seals. They come to shore in spring. Bears dig earth dens to stay cool in summer. In early winter, they make snow dens to wait for the new cubs to be born, until the sea ice forms. While on shore, polar bears may go four to seven months without eating.

Global warming is causing a dangerous situation for the bears. Sometimes, the sea ice does not form close to shore. The bears may be trapped on land, far from their main supply of food—the seals. If the winter stays warm, some bears may starve.

Polar Bear Provincial Park in northern Ontario, along the coast of Hudson Bay, and Wapusk National Park in Manitoba, are both protected places where polar bears live and breed.

The Arctic fox has a heavy white coat in winter. In summer, it is a grey colour.

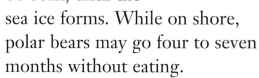

Do ◆ Discuss ◆ Discover

1. In a short paragraph, explain why the breeding grounds of migratory birds are important.

2. a) What is the purpose of national and provincial parks? Which national or provincial park is nearest to your home?

   b) Why do you think Polar Bear Provincial Park was chosen to be a protected environment?

Reader's Theatre – The Polar Bear

Reader 1: I am a polar bear. I live on the tundra and the ice, way up north.

Reader 2: You are Nanuk with a thick white coat that keeps you warm day and night.

Reader 3: You are a marine mammal with wide padded paws that help you swim and run around your home.

Reader 1: I am a polar bear. I track my prey without making a sound.

Reader 2: You are Nanuk searching for food in the water, ice, and snow.

Reader 3: You are a hunter patiently watching that air hole, waiting for a seal to appear.

Do ◆ Discuss ◆ Discover

1. In a small group, list all the information you have learned from this play about polar bears.

2. Look at the photographs and add any other information you have gained.

3. In your notebook, explain how a late freeze would affect the bears. Use the information from the text and your own ideas to support your answers.

Reader 1: I am a polar bear. I emerge from my snow den with two brand new cubs.

Reader 2: You are Nanuk keeping careful watch as your cubs roll and play.

Reader 3: You are a mother helping and guiding your cubs on their way.

Reader 1: I am a polar bear. I adapt to the way that my home is changing.

Reader 2: You are Nanuk roaming the icy Arctic and waiting for the late freeze.

Reader 3: You are a polar bear who sees the changes as you move from floe to floe.

Reader 1: I am a polar bear. I am Nanuk.

Fort Albany – A Hunting and Fishing Community

Fort Albany is a First Nations hunting and fishing community of about 1800 people. It is located on the shore of James Bay at the mouth of the Albany River.

A winter road connects Fort Albany to Moosonee, 128 kilometres to the southeast. It is open from January until late March. There is passenger, mail, and freight service to Fort Albany every day by air.

the region. Whitefish, trout, northern pike, pickerel, and other freshwater fish are found in the rivers and lakes. It is a wonderful place to live if you love to fish!

The best way to get to Fort Albany is by air.

People in Fort Albany use motor boats and canoes for hunting, fishing, and trapping in summer. Snowmobiles are the most common way of getting around the community in winter.

Wildlife is plentiful. There are geese, ducks, moose, caribou, bear, beaver, grouse, partridge, foxes, and other small animals in

A new school was built in the community.

Many people in Fort Albany are bilingual in Cree and English. Cree is taught in school, and students also learn traditional ways and skills. In spring, students get a two-week "hunting break" to take part in goose and moose hunting. A family feast of *niska* (goose) is held at the end of the hunting break.

Visit Fort Albany

1. Imagine you are travelling to Fort Albany on the summer supply barge. Describe what you see on shore as the barge travels slowly up the James Bay coast.

Natural Resources

The Hudson Bay Lowlands region has no developed mineral reserves or oil and gas wells. It is possible that oil or gas may be found there one day. Underneath Hudson Bay, there are layers of rock that are often associated with oil and gas fields.

There are several hydroelectric dams on rivers flowing into Hudson Bay and James Bay. Two large projects are found on the Nelson River in Manitoba and a tributary of the Moose River in Ontario.

From the observation tower, people can see for long distances across the flat tundra. These caribou pay no attention to the watchers.

Soils of the region are not suitable for agriculture. Most people depend on hunting and fishing for some of their food. Most other supplies arrive by airplane or ship. Hunting, fishing, and trapping for furs are part of the way of life for many people in the region.

Parts of the area are known for sports hunting and fishing. **Ecotourism** is growing in popularity. Eco-tourists are visitors who come to see the animal and bird life, natural vegetation, and landforms of the region.

First Nations guides accompany most tours. They know the region better than anyone. They make sure that conservation rules are followed.

This hydroelectric project on the Nelson River uses the force of the water to create electricity.

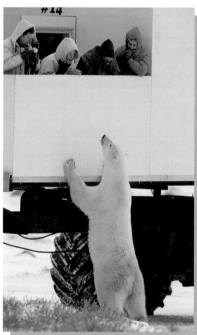

These visitors are watching polar bears from the safety of a tundra buggy.

The big lens on this camera is used to take pictures of distant birds and animals.

Do ◆ Discuss ◆ Discover

1. In a small group, discuss where the electricity from the hydroelectric projects may go.
2. What features of the region in which you live might be interesting to an ecotourist?
3. Discuss why supplies are brought in by airplane or ship.

Francis's Concern

My dad works for Environment Canada. He tries to make sure that the people who live in this region and visit here treat the land and its resources properly. He thinks it is important to keep the environment healthy. Both animals and humans need to live here together.

He has been going to meetings about the changes in the environment that can be caused by hydroelectric developments.

Large construction projects such as dams disturb the environment. The vegetation is removed, so mud washes into the river. This changes the habitats of fish, birds, and animals.

Huge numbers of waterbirds breed and nest in the wetlands of the region. If their habitat changes, the number of birds will decline.

I am concerned that projects such as hydroelectric dams must be carefully planned because of their effects on the environment.

Do ◆ Discuss ◆ Discover

1. a) Discuss the importance of suitable nesting and breeding areas for birds and animals in the Hudson Bay Lowlands region.
   b) Brainstorm possible questions you would ask at a construction-planning meeting in this region.

Chapter 6

Knowledge and Understanding

1. Draw a region organizer similar to the one you did on page 69 of Chapter 5. Write the title "The Hudson Bay Lowlands" at the top. Use information from this chapter and your notes to fill in every area of the organizer. Put it into your notebook.

2. Identify vocabulary from this chapter to add to the vocabulary section of your notebook. Draw diagrams or sketches to help you remember the words and their meanings.

3. Design a coin to illustrate and represent the importance of animal life in the Hudson Bay Lowlands region.

Inquiry/Research and Communication Skills

4. Research an animal found in the Hudson Bay Lowlands region. Follow the research model on page 14. Create a mobile that shows each of the following:

   a) title for the mobile
   b) picture of the animal, bird, or sea life
   c) where it lives
   d) what it eats
   e) why it might be in danger

Map, Globe, and Graphic Skills

5. Create a poster to attract fishers to one of the rivers in the region.

Application

6. In groups of three, create a script for a radio or television commercial promoting the protection of Canada's wetlands. Share your work with one other group.

Internet Connection

7. Go to www.duvaleducation. com/ourcountrycanada2. Click on the link to Parks to learn about Polar Bear Provincial Park and Wapusk National Park. Create a Venn diagram comparing the two parks. In your notebook, write two questions about each park that you would like to ask a friend.

The Canada Project

1. Find the outline map of Canada you started at the end of Chapter 2. Colour the Hudson Bay Lowlands region. Label the provinces/territories that are in the Hudson Bay Lowlands region. Add important information about the Hudson Bay Lowlands region to your map. (Use the maps on page 70 and inside the front and back covers of the text to help.)

2. Create a tourism brochure for your province/territory that focuses on something special relating to the natural environment. Put it into your scrapbook or shoebox.

Chapter 7
The St. Lawrence Lowlands

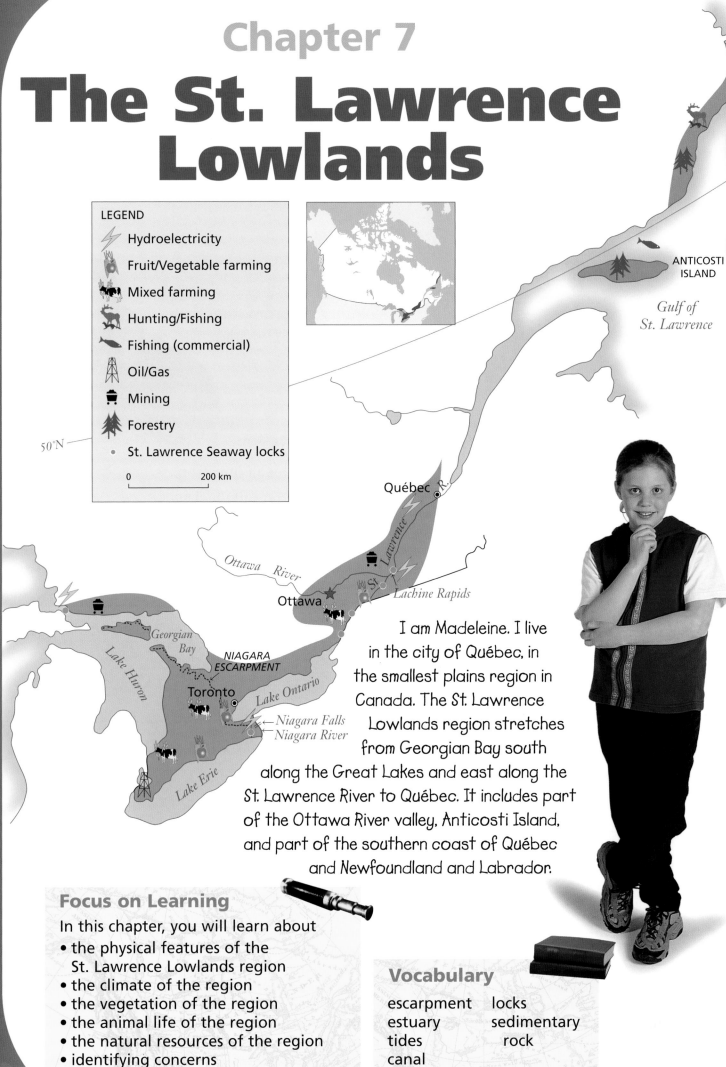

LEGEND

- Hydroelectricity
- Fruit/Vegetable farming
- Mixed farming
- Hunting/Fishing
- Fishing (commercial)
- Oil/Gas
- Mining
- Forestry
- St. Lawrence Seaway locks

0   200 km

50°N

ANTICOSTI ISLAND

Gulf of St. Lawrence

Québec

Ottawa River

Ottawa

St. Lawrence

Lachine Rapids

Georgian Bay

Lake Huron

NIAGARA ESCARPMENT

Toronto

Lake Ontario

Niagara Falls
Niagara River

Lake Erie

I am Madeleine. I live in the city of Québec, in the smallest plains region in Canada. The St. Lawrence Lowlands region stretches from Georgian Bay south along the Great Lakes and east along the St. Lawrence River to Québec. It includes part of the Ottawa River valley, Anticosti Island, and part of the southern coast of Québec and Newfoundland and Labrador.

Focus on Learning

In this chapter, you will learn about
- the physical features of the St. Lawrence Lowlands region
- the climate of the region
- the vegetation of the region
- the animal life of the region
- the natural resources of the region
- identifying concerns

Vocabulary

escarpment   locks
estuary   sedimentary
tides   rock
canal

Physical Features

The St. Lawrence Lowlands region is made up of plains and some hills. The rivers in the region drain into the five Great Lakes and the St. Lawrence River. Particles of earth called sediment are carried by rivers and streams. They have formed a plain with deep, fertile soils.

The region is much lower than the surrounding areas. In parts of the region, the way up to higher ground is very steep. It is like a long rock cliff. This is called an **escarpment**. An escarpment is a barrier to travel. A road, railroad, or boat has to make its way up a steep incline to continue onto the higher land.

The St. Lawrence River flows into the Gulf of St. Lawrence through an **estuary**. This is where the mouth of a large river flows into the ocean. Salt water from the ocean mingles with the fresh water of a river.

The water level in the estuary and Gulf of St. Lawrence east of Québec is raised and lowered twice a day by tides.

The fertile soils of the plains are good for farming.

Tides are caused by the force of the Moon's gravity pulling on the waters of the Earth.

The plains area along the St. Lawrence River is narrow in some places.

The Niagara Escarpment

The part of the Niagara Escarpment that is in Ontario is 725 kilometres long. It runs from Queenston on the Niagara River to Manitoulin Island in Georgian Bay. In the highest place, it is 335 metres high. The Niagara River flows over the escarpment at Niagara Falls.

Do ◆ Discuss ◆ Discover

1. How might people 200 years ago have dealt with travelling up and down an escarpment?
2. Predict what crops might be grown in this region of fertile soil. (You'll find out for sure later in the chapter!)

St. Lawrence Seaway

The St. Lawrence River has been a major water route since earliest times. Aboriginal people, European explorers, and settlers all travelled on it.

Large boats could not go farther upstream than the Lachine Rapids in Québec until the first canal was built.

Canals were built to straighten and deepen the river's channel. Then larger boats could pass through. Later, **locks** were built to raise and lower boats in places where elevation changed greatly. Different parts of the waterway were improved at different times.

Since 1959, ships have been able to travel 3790 kilometres inland to Thunder Bay on the west side of Lake Superior.

Boat traffic on the Seaway today includes everything from huge tankers and cargo ships to tiny pleasure boats.

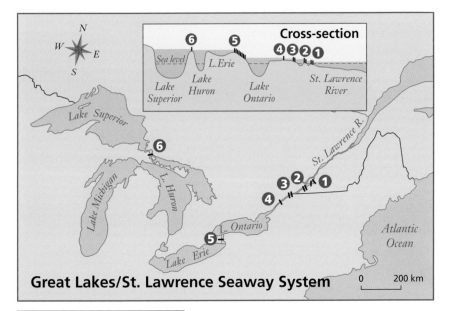

Great Lakes/St. Lawrence Seaway System

Lake Superior is the second-largest freshwater lake in the world.

LEGEND
Seaway Locks
1. St. Lambert and Côte Ste. Catherine
2. Beauharnois (2)
3. Snell and Eisenhower
4. Iroquois
5. Welland Canal (8)
6. Sault Ste. Marie

The Seaway looks like a water highway crossing the countryside.

Do ◆ Discuss ◆ Discover

Work with a partner to research the history of the St. Lawrence Seaway.

1. a) Who used the waterway first?
   b) When were the first canals or locks built?
   c) When were the last built?
2. Create a timeline in the form of a river to display the dates in sequence.

Changes Along the St. Lawrence

The early explorers used the St. Lawrence River system to explore and settle in Canada. Over time, many people came to live in cities and towns near the St. Lawrence River and the Great Lakes. Many people live in this area and rely on this river system for their work, rest, and play.

European settlers came to North America by ship and used canoes to go further inland. Trails from the towns led *coureurs de bois* to the valuable furs for trading.

European ships and boats from local areas brought more goods and people to settle along the St. Lawrence River system. More roads and railroads were established.

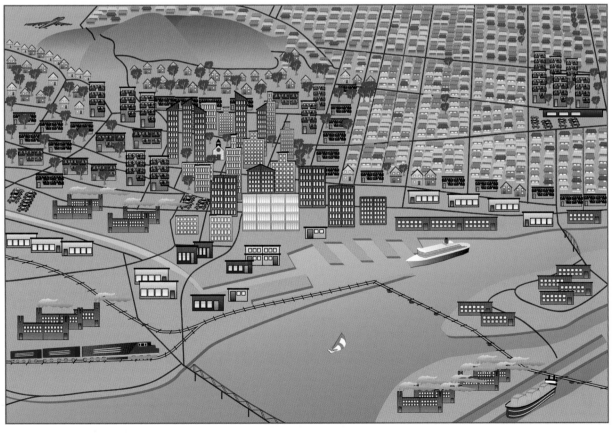

Today, people along the St. Lawrence River system still depend on the lakes and river for their transportation, economic, and recreational needs. Railroads, highways, and airports have been built to serve the needs of people living in this area.

Locks

There are locks on several sections of the St. Lawrence Seaway. Locks work like an elevator. Watertight "rooms" with gates let ships in at one level. Then the water level changes so they can exit at a different level. The following example shows a boat travelling downstream through a set of locks.

These ships are passing through the locks in Thorold, Ontario.

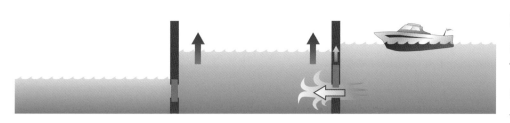

Step 1: The boat approaches the lock. The gates at both ends of the lock are closed and water is allowed to flow into it. The water level rises to match the river.

Step 2: The first gate opens and the boat enters the lock. Then the gate closes again.

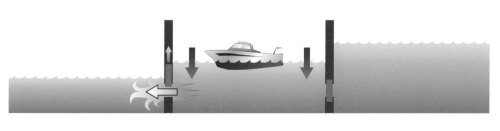

Step 3: When both gates are closed, water is released downstream to the river. The level of water in the lock is made equal to the river below.

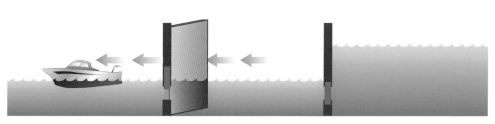

Step 4: The downstream gate is opened and the boat travels out of the lock into the river. The gate closes again.

Niagara – A Natural Wonder

Did you know that Niagara Falls has moved? When the falls were formed at the end of the last ice age, they were 11 kilometres farther downstream!

Water pours off the falls at a rate of 14 million litres per minute. Water rushing over the Horseshoe Falls has broken away the rocks under the falls a little at a time. Erosion changes the position of Niagara Falls 1.2 metres per year.

Niagara Falls is made of three layers of different rocks: dolomite, shale, and limestone. The top layer is dolomite. It is a hard, thick layer of **sedimentary rock**.

The shale and limestone layers underneath are softer sedimentary rocks. Sedimentary rocks are formed when many layers of particles carried by water have settled on each other and hardened into rock.

The water of the falls flows over the top and lands in the river far below. It splashes back over the face of the falls. Slowly, bits of the softer rock wear away. The dolomite layer on top is undercut. Eventually, another piece of the top layer breaks off and falls into the river. The shape and position of the falls change again.

Niagara Falls is not the highest waterfall in the world, but the greatest volume of water pours over it.

Do ◆ Discuss ◆ Discover

1. In groups of three, plan an experiment that you could do to demonstrate how the position of Niagara Falls changes. What materials would you need? What steps would you follow? Are there any special concerns about safety or getting permission for the demonstration? What are they? You do not have to carry out the experiment.

Climate

Visitors enjoy the water on hot summer days.

This region has hot temperatures and humid weather during the summer. It has one of the longest growing seasons in Canada. The winters are cool and often snowy.

The St. Lawrence Lowlands region has several parts. The part closer to the Atlantic Ocean is colder than the part near the Great Lakes. It is farther north. Storms from the Atlantic Ocean are also more frequent there.

The place farthest south in Canada is Middle Island near Pelee Island in Lake Erie. It is at 42° N latitude. The southern border of most of Canada is at the 49th parallel, or 49° N.

Precipitation can come as heavy snowfall in some parts of the region.

Vegetation

The St. Lawrence Lowlands region has old and new forests. The forests contain many kinds of deciduous and coniferous trees. Trees grow to be large because there is plenty of moisture and heat in summer.

Deciduous trees such as birch, maple, and walnut grow in the region. Coniferous trees such as pines, spruce, and fir are also present. Many shrubs, flowers, and grasses grow abundantly.

The provincial flower of Ontario is the trillium. It blooms in forests throughout the region in early spring.

Animal Life

Many types of animals live in the St. Lawrence Lowlands region. Land animals include white-tailed deer, squirrels, coyotes, moose, wolves, snowshoe hares, and lynx. Warblers, red-winged blackbirds, and bluebirds are a few of the many species of birds that make their homes in this region. Many migrating species spend a short time in the region on their way to their summer and winter homes.

This Northern Flicker has made a nest in a tree.

Natural Resources

The two most important natural resources of the St. Lawrence Lowlands region are the good farming land and the waterway system. This narrow area of plains has fertile soil, a mild climate, and plenty of water. Many kinds of fruits and vegetables are grown there. Peaches, apples, and grapes are only a few well-known products.

Apple orchards need many frost-free days to produce ripe fruit for sale.

Dairy farming is an important industry in the region.

The Great Lakes and the St. Lawrence River form a waterway system over half of the width of Canada! The waterway has been used for transporting goods and people for thousands of years.

Huge ocean-going container ships pass farming communities along the St. Lawrence River.

The St. Lawrence Lowlands region in Ontario and Québec contains a huge number of manufacturing industries. They produce countless products. They use natural resources from many different regions, so transportation is important.

Many Canadians benefit from the huge supplies of fresh water in the St. Lawrence Lowlands region. Water is used for drinking, cleaning, manufacturing, recreation, agriculture, transportation, and creating hydroelectricity.

Do ◆ Discuss ◆ Discover

1. What kinds of farming and farm products come from the St. Lawrence Lowlands region? Remember to think about the different parts of the region. List five different types in your notebook.

2. List the different uses and benefits of the St. Lawrence Seaway system. Identify how many of these affect you personally. Briefly describe how.

St. Lawrence Lowlands Arts

Quilts are a fabric art. They are made of many pieces of cloth sewn together to form a pattern. Many quilts show an abstract pattern. Others present a picture made of many colours and textures of cloth.

Patterns may use the same pieces repeated in different ways, or different pieces repeated in a regular way. Contrast is important.

Envelopes, created by Bridget O'Flaherty, Perth, ON

The Road Not Taken, created by Bridget O'Flaherty, Perth, ON

Patterns

Dark and light and dark
Ripple and echo
Like two tom-toms and a flute
Calling across the far lake water.
And moonlight shines on the boat dock
Of your last summer cottage night.

Tomorrow you will drive
And drive through miles
    of forest, fireweed, smoke stacks, rail cars,
    gravel pits, side roads, dusty school buses,
And fast food outlets.

To the familiar streets of home
The familiar ring of the telephone
The washing machine groaning lowly
And your own bed back at last.

— B. Gibbs

Do ◆ Discuss ◆ Discover

1. Discuss with a partner how the image in the quilt *The Road Not Taken* represents the St. Lawrence Lowlands region.
2. Create a work of art based on pattern. You can choose to use sounds, colours, textures, or images to make your pattern.

A Farming Community

The cranberry is a wetland fruit that grows on trailing vines, similar to a strawberry.

For many years, cranberries have been used as food by Aboriginal people. Pemmican is prepared with lean, dried strips of meat pounded into paste and mixed with animal fat, cranberries, and grains. Cranberries are also used in ceremonies and as medicine.

The Wahta Mohawks came to the Muskoka area in 1881 from Oka, Québec. They began harvesting cranberries commercially from the bog shortly after their move.

The cranberry vines grow well in the special combination of sand, peat, gravel, and clay in the region. The growing season goes from April to November, and the cranberry harvest takes place once a year in the fall.

There are two ways to harvest cranberries. The most common way is the wet harvest. Cranberries have air inside them, so they float in water. The beds are flooded and the cranberries are removed from the vines using water reels. Water reels are like egg beaters. They make the cranberries come off the vines and float to the top of the water. Then the cranberries are collected.

The other way to harvest cranberries is called dry harvesting. This method does not use water. Walk-behind machines rake the berries off the vines into boxes or bags.

Cranberries can be used fresh or frozen. They are also made into juice and used in cooking and baking.

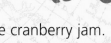

Hands On!

This simple recipe can be used to make cranberry jam. You will need the help of an adult.

You will need

- 1 cup of water
- 1 cup of orange juice
- 3 cups of cranberries
- 3 cups of sugar

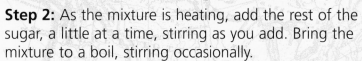

Step 1: Pour the water and orange juice into a large pot. Add the cranberries and one cup of sugar.

Step 2: As the mixture is heating, add the rest of the sugar, a little at a time, stirring as you add. Bring the mixture to a boil, stirring occasionally.

Step 3: Reduce the heat to medium-low and simmer. Stir occasionally until it thickens (about 20–30 minutes).

Step 4: Carefully pour the hot mixture into a blender or food processor. Pulse the mixture until it is almost pureed. Now the jam is ready to be canned.

Step 5: Pour the jam into sterilized jars, seal them, and turn them upside down. Cover the jars with a cloth and let them cool completely before turning them right side up. Store them in a cool place. After opening the jars, any leftover jam should be refrigerated.

Madeleine's Concern

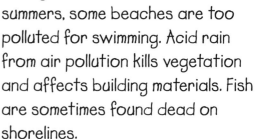

WARNING
UNSAFE FOR SWIMMING
Water temporarily POLLUTED
because of high bacteria levels
which may pose a risk to your health

If you find
a needle
Do not touch it!
Tell a lifeguard or
a parks attendant

My aunt plans educational trips of the waterways in this region. For example, she guides boat tours to see the whales in the Gulf of St. Lawrence.

Many industries are located near the St. Lawrence River system. Factories and industries are a source of water and air pollution. Sometimes, smoke is heavy and dark in this area.

The population of the St. Lawrence Lowlands region is very high. There are more people per square kilometre than in any other region of Canada. Automobiles, homes, and businesses all produce smoke and waste.

The people in this region are concerned about the pollution levels. During some summers, some beaches are too polluted for swimming. Acid rain from air pollution kills vegetation and affects building materials. Fish are sometimes found dead on shorelines.

Everybody needs to help in order to make a difference. I am concerned that as the population continues to grow, these problems will increase. We need to plan for the future to prevent this.

Do ◆ Discuss ◆ Discover

1. Discuss possible reasons why this region has so many people and industries.
2. Discuss the many uses of the waterway and the effects that large numbers of people and industries have on it.

Chapter 7

Knowledge and Understanding

1. Draw a region organizer similar to the one you did on page 79 of Chapter 6. Write the title "The St. Lawrence Lowlands" at the top. Use information from this chapter and your notes to fill in every area of the organizer. Put it into your notebook.

2. Identify vocabulary from this chapter to add to the vocabulary section of your notebook. Draw diagrams or sketches to help you remember the words and their meanings.

3. Draw your own diagram of how a lock works. Include an explanation in your own words.

Inquiry/Research and Communication Skills

4. Keep a one-day journal of the ways water is used around your home. Research how you can reduce the use of water in your home. Follow the research model on page 14. Discuss your findings with two other students in your class.

5. Research Niagara Falls. Create a one-page magazine advertisement with pictures and information of the different places and activities in Niagara Falls.

Map, Globe, and Graphic Skills

6. Sketch or trace the St. Lawrence Seaway diagram on page 82. Label all the parts and put it into your notebook.

7. On an outline map of the region, locate and label major cities along the St. Lawrence Seaway. Also identify and label the major transportation routes in this region. Include ship, air, road, and railroad routes.

Application

8. Look at page 83. In a small group, discuss the changes to the area around the St. Lawrence River. In your notebook, create a timeline that shows the impact an increase in population has had on the river. Add other uses of the river based on your own knowledge and experience. You may use pictures, symbols, or sentences.

The Canada Project

1. Find the outline map of Canada you started at the end of Chapter 2. Colour the St. Lawrence Lowlands region. Label the provinces/territories that are in the St. Lawrence Lowlands region. Add important information about the St. Lawrence Lowlands region to your map. (Use the maps on page 80 and inside the front and back covers of the text to help.)

2. On an outline map of your province/territory, locate and label all major rivers, lakes, and bodies of water. On the back of the map or a separate piece of paper, create a chart listing the major waterways and the uses and benefits of each. Put it into your scrapbook or shoebox.

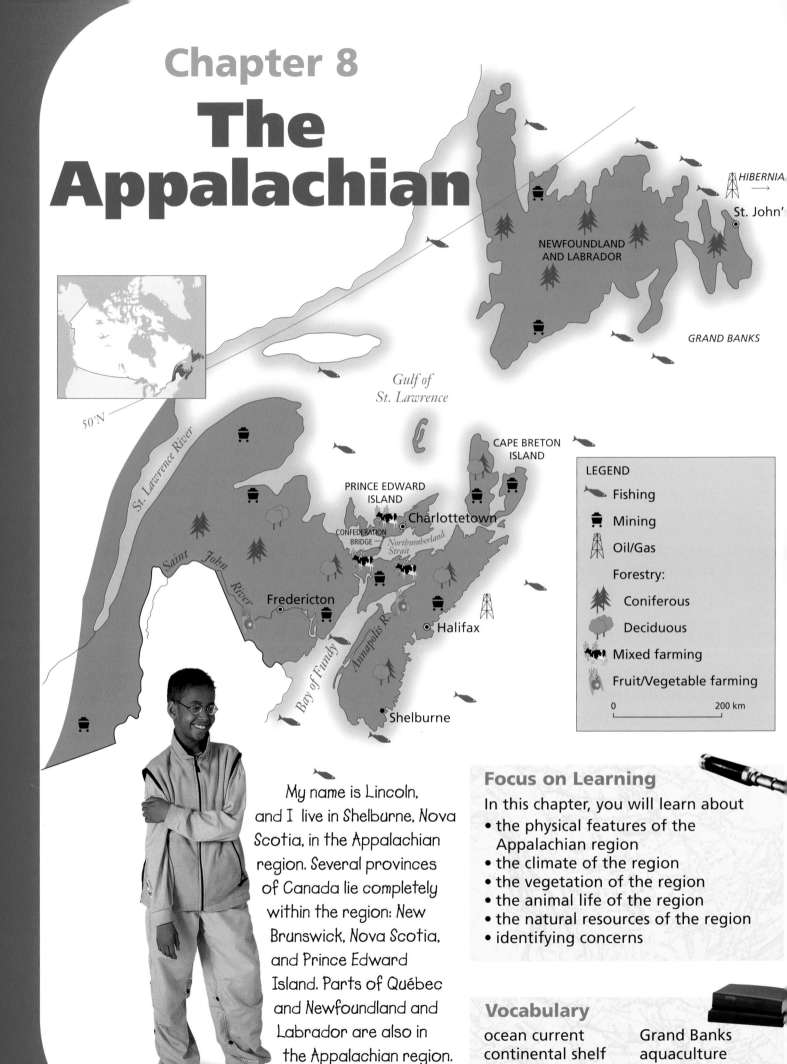

Chapter 8
The Appalachian

HIBERNIA →

St. John'

NEWFOUNDLAND
AND LABRADOR

GRAND BANKS

Gulf of
St. Lawrence

50°N

St. Lawrence River

CAPE BRETON
ISLAND

PRINCE EDWARD
ISLAND

Charlottetown

CONFEDERATION
BRIDGE

Northumberland
Strait

Saint John River

Fredericton

Bay of Fundy

Annapolis R.

Halifax

Shelburne

LEGEND

- Fishing
- Mining
- Oil/Gas

Forestry:

- Coniferous
- Deciduous

- Mixed farming
- Fruit/Vegetable farming

0   200 km

My name is Lincoln, and I live in Shelburne, Nova Scotia, in the Appalachian region. Several provinces of Canada lie completely within the region: New Brunswick, Nova Scotia, and Prince Edward Island. Parts of Québec and Newfoundland and Labrador are also in the Appalachian region.

Focus on Learning

In this chapter, you will learn about
- the physical features of the Appalachian region
- the climate of the region
- the vegetation of the region
- the animal life of the region
- the natural resources of the region
- identifying concerns

Vocabulary

ocean current
continental shelf

Grand Banks
aquaculture

Physical Features

The Appalachian region is part of a low range of mountains. Scientists call these mountains old. They were created long before the mountains of the Cordillera region. They have been worn down by erosion over millions of years.

Rocky cliffs, islands, bays, protected harbours, and beaches are found along the coast.

The region faces the Atlantic Ocean. It has thousands of kilometres of sea coast. The bigger islands within this region are Prince Edward Island, Newfoundland, and Cape Breton Island. Waves, ocean currents, and tides erode the cliffs and form beaches in the region.

An ocean current is a stream of moving water within a larger body of water. A drifting boat caught in an ocean current can be carried many kilometres along a coast or out to sea.

Off the shores of the Appalachian region, the ocean floor slants gradually downward. Then it drops off abruptly into a deep trench. The slanting ocean floor is called the **continental shelf**. Southeast of Newfoundland and Labrador lie several shallower parts of the continental shelf. They are called the **Grand Banks**, and they are famous as a fishing ground.

The plains and valley areas of the region have fertile soils in some places. In other places, they are rocky or boggy.

People who swim or fish in the ocean must learn about the tides and ocean currents in order to be safe.

A green valley along the Saint John River in New Brunswick

Do ◆ Discuss ◆ Discover

1. In a small group, create a pamphlet about the tides and the ocean currents to alert tourists who are visiting the beaches of the Appalachian region.

Tides

Tides are changes in the level of the water caused by the pull of the Moon's gravity.

The water rises for about six hours, as it flows towards the shore. Then the water begins to flow back out to sea again.

At low tide, these boats along the Bay of Fundy rest on the ocean bottom. As the water rises, they will float again.

This also lasts about six hours. The difference between the water level at high tide and at low tide is called the tidal range.

Tides move the waters of the Earth. They bring fresh food and oxygen to plants and animals living near shore, and they take away waste products. The tides in the Annapolis, Nova Scotia, area power a generating station that creates electricity for the area.

The Bay of Fundy has the highest tides in the world. The difference between high tide and low tide can be as much as 15 metres. Compare this to the height of a house roof!

Climate

The climate in the Appalachian region varies. The summers may be cool or warm and rainy. The long winters have a lot of precipitation. Precipitation ranges from about 1100 millimetres to 1400 millimetres per year.

Plentiful rainfall helps forests to grow.

Ice storms and snowstorms are frequent on the Atlantic coast.

The Northumberland Strait between Prince Edward Island and the mainland freezes in the winter. Fierce storms called gales are common in winter. Winter wind speeds may reach 100 kilometres per hour on the islands and shoreline.

Winds over 50 kilometres to 60 kilometres per hour are considered to be gale force winds.

Do ◆ Discuss ◆ Discover

1. Do an Internet search to learn more about gales and the Northumberland Strait. In a small group, create a weather report warning travellers of a fierce storm coming the next day. Read your report out loud to another group.

The Confederation Bridge

The Confederation Bridge was built to connect Prince Edward Island and New Brunswick. It was officially opened on May 31, 1997. The bridge is 12.9 kilometres long.

The Confederation Bridge was designed to withstand the severe weather in the Northumberland Strait. For many years, engineers studied the effects that the tides, gales, and sea ice would have on the structure. For example, they designed the bridge supports to split apart ice floes that hit them as they move through the Strait.

A weather station monitors weather conditions on the bridge 24 hours a day. It reports wind speed, wind direction, air temperature, road temperature, humidity, and precipitation.

When the weather is bad, the bridge is closed to traffic. People must then take the ferry across the Strait, just as they did before the bridge was completed.

The Confederation Bridge is the longest bridge ever built over ice-covered water.

Do ◆ Discuss ◆ Discover

1. Why do you think people wanted to have the Confederation Bridge to link Prince Edward Island with New Brunswick?

2. Now that you know about the climate in this region, why did the engineers spend so much time designing the bridge?

Go to www.duvaleducation.com/ourcountrycanada2. Click on the link to the Confederation Bridge to see the history of building this bridge.

Vegetation

Mixed forests of oak, red maple, spruce, and white pine grow in valleys and lower areas.

Much of the mainland Appalachian region is forested. Coniferous trees grow in the higher areas, both inland and on the coast. Forests of black and white spruce and balsam fir are found there. Hardwood forests of white and yellow birch, beech, and sugar maple once grew in the higher areas. They have been almost completely logged.

Trees grow slowly in the Appalachian region. The climate is often harsh. The soil is rocky or not fertile in many places.

The mainland Appalachian region is home to many different species of animals. Mammals include white-tailed deer, fox, snowshoe hare, coyote, mink, otter, muskrat, porcupine, beaver, and raccoon.

Newfoundland and Labrador once had fewer types of land animals than other parts of the region. Many were introduced to the region, including moose, caribou, snowshoe hare, and squirrel.

Great blue herons and many species of ducks, shorebirds, and waterfowl can be found along the beaches and in marshes and lagoons.

Bonaventure Island is a migratory bird sanctuary. It is home to puffins, gulls, and razorbills.

Thousands of seabirds, such as puffins, gulls, and auks, breed on rocky cliffs and islands.

Whales are found in the Gulf of St. Lawrence, but they have been affected by polluted waters.

Animal Life

In the past, this area has been one of the richest ocean fishing grounds in the world. Cod fish used to be very plentiful. Today, smaller numbers of fish are found in this area.

Grey seals and harbour seals can be found in estuaries and harbours.

Do ◆ Discuss ◆ Discover

1. a) Choose one animal from this region to research.

   b) Write a postcard fact sheet on the animal. Place important information about the animal on one side and include a picture on the other.

   c) Write four Who Am I? clues for the animal.

   d) With a partner, play the Who Am I? game and then share your postcard with them.

Natural Resources

In the past, the Appalachian region has been known for its coal mines and its fishing. Many of the coal mines of the region are now closed because the costs to operate them became greater. The fishing industry has also become weaker as ocean fish become fewer.

Some zinc and lead, potash, salt, asbestos, copper, and gold are mined in the region. There are also two offshore oil fields. One is on the continental shelf near Nova Scotia. The other is on the Grand Banks near Newfoundland and Labrador.

The oil field on the Grand Banks is called Hibernia.

Cod, salmon, pollock, halibut, redfish, herring, swordfish, sole, flounder, haddock, clams, oysters, scallops, and lobster are all harvested in the Atlantic region. The government makes laws to help conserve the fish stocks.

The government prevents other countries from fishing closer than 200 nautical miles from Canada's shore. (A nautical mile is about 1850 metres.) The government does this to protect this valuable resource.

There are two types of commercial fishing. One is inshore fishing. Small boats, used mainly by families, harvest cod and lobster for local restaurants and tourist areas. They operate from May to September.

The government controls the number of fish that can be caught so the fishing industry will continue to provide food and jobs for Canadians.

Large fishing boats, or trawlers, go out into the ocean in fleets to catch the fish. This is offshore fishing. They drag steel mesh nets along the ocean floor to scoop up fish. Large fishing boats can clean and process the fish at sea. They can operate year round.

Do ◆ Discuss ◆ Discover

1. Why would the government protect the fishing industry by preventing other countries from fishing inside the 200-nautical-mile limit?

A Fishing Community

I live in Shelburne, Nova Scotia. This community was founded in the southwest corner of the province in the 1780s.

In 2007, Shelburne celebrated its 100th birthday as a town. It has a population of about 2000. Its natural harbour is considered the third-best in the world.

Shelburne began as a fishing and shipbuilding centre. Many historic buildings still exist. Tourists come to see what an Atlantic fishing town looked like in the past.

Fishing is still very important. However, today we are involved in a new industry called aquaculture. Aquaculture combines fishing and farming, because fish are raised like a crop. Read the following article about aquaculture that was in my school newspaper.

A new fish story

For the last few years, fishers have been discouraged by the news that our ocean fish stocks are being slowly used up. The government wanted us to lower the number of fish we caught on the Grand Banks and off the coast of our province. But all over the country, people are demanding fish as a source of food. We have to find new ways to provide fish.

What is aquaculture? It is fish farming. The workers create a series of containers, similar to large pools. These containers hold the fish at the different stages of their development.

Aquaculture ponds at a fish farm

Aquaculture, just like farming, involves the seeding, feeding, and harvesting of fish. Fish eggs are hatched, the fish are fed, and when they are full grown, they are harvested. Fish have been farmed in other parts of the world for many centuries. However, it is a new industry here—only a few decades old. Fish farmers here are raising blue mussels, European oysters, steelhead salmon, and sea scallops.

Many people are excited about aquaculture. It is like farming the sea, and it's an alternative to fishing. The opportunities for selling fish to other countries are excellent. Aquaculture should also provide many future jobs.

Go to www.duvaleducation.com/ourcountrycanada2. Click on the link to Resources to learn more about aquaculture.

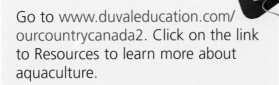

Visit Shelburne

1. Plan a tour of Shelburne. Write an itinerary to put into your notebook of the places you will go. Don't forget lunch!

The Newfoundland Cod

Basking in the sun
One summer day
Was a giant cod
At Fortune Bay.
I stepped on this cod
In Newfoundland,
Stepped on its head
As it slept on the sand.

It sprang to its tail
By the sunny sea.
It bugged its eyes
And screamed at me:
"Kiss me or tickle me,
Hug me or pickle me,
Jiggle me, wiggle me,
Suddenly squiggle me.
Take me and flake me,
Shake me and bake me.
Batter me, fry me,
Poach me or dry me.
But keep your stinking
Feet away
From codfish sunning
At Fortune Bay!"

As it wiggled its way
Back into the sea
A monster wave
Washed over me.
It spanked me
With a dozen whacks
From Newfoundland
To Halifax.

And...
Never, ever
Since that day
Have I stepped on a cod
At Fortune Bay.

— Robert Heidbreder

Do ◆ Discuss ◆ Discover

Read the poem on this page and discuss the following questions.

1. a) Why might this be called a "nonsense poem"?

   b) Give examples of the way the author uses sounds to create a certain effect in the poem.

   c) Give examples of images the author uses to help you "see" the scene.

Lincoln's Concern

My mom is a marine biologist. We live in Shelburne. When she comes home at night, we like to talk. Often, we discuss how her day went and the things I have learned in school. The other day, we discussed the way the numbers of fish have declined. It is very difficult for people to make a living fishing.

My mom had a lot of information about why the fish stocks were getting so low. She explained that trawlers catch both young and adult fish. If younger fish are not left to become adults, no new fish will be born.

Many large fishing companies take fish out of the same area. Trawlers come from a number of different countries to compete with Canadian companies for fish in the ocean.

Regulations have become stricter. However, some kinds of fish and shellfish will take a long time to increase their numbers. This problem affects everyone in my town.

The young people in my community are concerned about the future of the fishing industry and the fish in the Atlantic Ocean.

Do ◆ Discuss ◆ Discover

1. Discuss reasons that explain the declining numbers of fish. (Use the information from above and earlier in the chapter.)
2. Discuss the different ways lower numbers of fish could affect a community such as Shelburne.

Chapter 8

Knowledge and Understanding

1. Draw a region organizer similar to the one you did on page 91 of Chapter 7. Write the title "The Appalachian" at the top. Use information from this chapter and your notes to fill in every area of the organizer. Put it into your notebook.

2. Identify vocabulary from this chapter to add to the vocabulary section of your notebook. Draw diagrams or sketches to help you remember the words and their meanings.

3. Create a web about the Grand Banks and put it into your notebook.

Inquiry/Research and Communication Skills

4. Research the different methods inshore and offshore fishing vessels use to catch fish. Follow the research model on page 14. Draw and label a picture of each method.

Application

5. Listen to some traffic reports on the radio. Write the script for a traffic report for the Confederation Bridge on a windy winter day. Record or read aloud your traffic report for your classmates.

Internet Connection

6. Go to www.duvaleducation.com/ourcountrycanada2. Click on the link to the Confederation Bridge. Work in a small group to create a fact card (like a baseball card) for the bridge statistics. Include facts such as how long it is and how many people travel on it. Remember to include a picture of the bridge on the front.

The Canada Project

1. Find the outline map of Canada you started at the end of Chapter 2. Colour the Appalachian region. Label the provinces/territories that are in the Appalachian region. Add important information about the Appalachian region to your map. (Use the maps on page 92 and inside the front and back covers of the text to help.)

2. Identify a natural land formation created by water or wind in your province/territory. Find a picture or draw your own illustration of the landform. On the back, write a short paragraph explaining how the landform was created. Put it into your scrapbook or shoebox.

3. Put all the organizers you have filled in for regions in your province/territory into your scrapbook or shoebox.

Chapter 9
Our Provinces and Territories

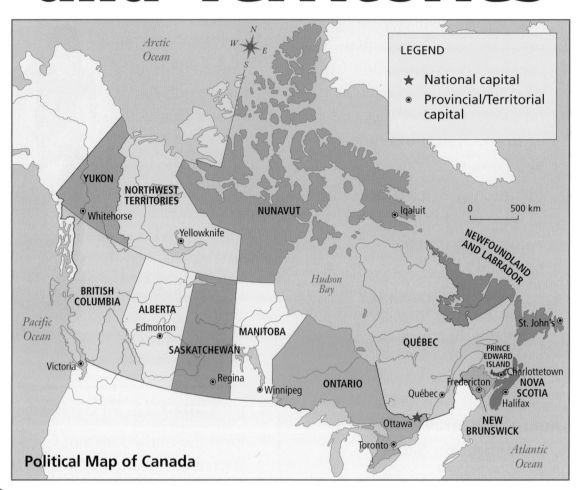

LEGEND

★ National capital

◉ Provincial/Territorial capital

0   500 km

Political Map of Canada

We have been looking at our country, Canada, in different ways. We have looked at the seven physical regions and at our rich natural resources.

The map on this page shows Canada's political divisions. Canada is divided into ten provinces and three territories. Each has a capital city, where its government meets.

Focus on Learning

In this chapter, you will learn about
- describing political regions
- our national capital
- map reading: grids
- the provinces and territories of Canada
- map reading: boundaries

Vocabulary

province

territory

capital city

grid

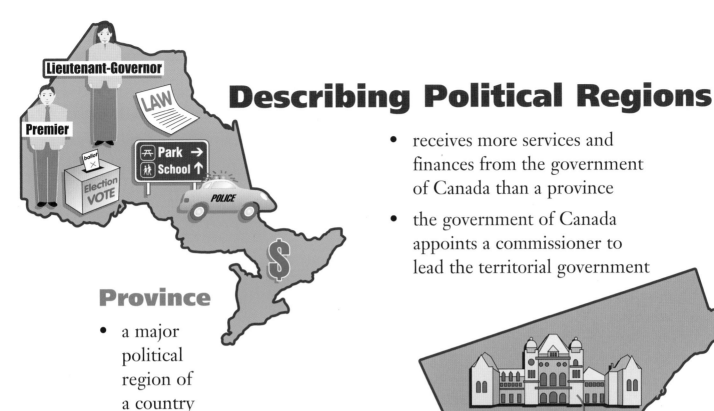

Describing Political Regions

- receives more services and finances from the government of Canada than a province

- the government of Canada appoints a commissioner to lead the territorial government

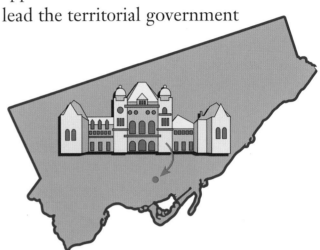

Province

- a major political region of a country

- residents elect provincial government and premier

- provincial government makes laws and provides services

- residents pay for government and services through taxes

- some services and finances come from the government of Canada

Territory

- a political region with a small population in a large area

- residents elect the territorial government

- territorial government makes some laws and provides some services

- residents pay for government and some services through taxes

Capital City

- a city in a country, province, or territory containing the government buildings

- national capital of Canada is Ottawa, Ontario

- provincial capital of Ontario is Toronto

Do ◆ Discuss ◆ Discover

1. Add the three terms on this page to the vocabulary section of your notebook.

2. Find the outline map of Canada from Chapter 1 where you labelled the provinces and territories and the places from which the seven children came. Now add the capital cities of each province and territory and Ottawa to this map.

3. Playing games will help you learn the names of the provinces and territories and their capital cities. Invent a simple game with a partner and play it together. Exchange games with another pair of students.

Our National Capital

Ottawa is the capital of Canada. The federal government meets there. It deals with concerns and makes laws that affect the whole country. Members of the federal government are known as Members of Parliament, or MPs.

Thousands of people come to the Parliament Buildings in Ottawa to celebrate Canada Day.

The Byward Market is one of the oldest parts of Ottawa. It is famous for shopping and entertainment.

The National Gallery of Canada has a wonderful collection of art. There are many museums in Ottawa.

The Rideau Canal is used for skating in the winter and boating in the summer.

Do ◆ Discuss ◆ Discover

1. Draw a four-season picture of how the Rideau Canal can be used for fun and recreation year round.

2. On a page in your notebook, create a list of reasons to visit Ottawa. Leave room to add more reasons as you read further in this chapter.

Map Reading: Grids

Look carefully at the globe. Notice the set of lines that runs east–west, parallel to the equator. These are called lines of latitude.

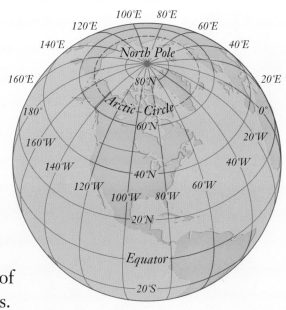

A second set of lines runs north–south. These lines are not parallel. They are farthest apart at the equator and meet at the North Pole and the South Pole. These are called lines of longitude.

Places on Earth can be named or described using their position of latitude and longitude. The two sets of lines form a **grid**. A grid divides up an area into blocks.

Maps provide grids to help you locate places on them. A grid is like a table made up of columns and rows. The columns are identified with alphabet letters and the rows are identified with numbers. The numbers and letters on the grid help you name the blocks. This is a sample of a grid.

To find an item on a grid, put one finger of your right hand on the correct letter block. Put one finger of your left hand on the correct number block. Slide your right finger down the column. At the same time, slide your left finger across the row. Where the two fingers meet is the item on the grid.

Do ◆ Discuss ◆ Discover

1. What symbol is in block A2? What symbol is in block C3?
2. Make a grid, adding your own symbols or pictures. Make up five questions about items on your grid. Work with a partner to practise finding symbols on each other's grids.

105

Touring Ottawa

Today, we are going to tour the city of Ottawa. All the sights of the city are close together and easy to find. We will work in teams to follow the scavenger hunt clues on the next page. Follow the map, and visit some of the sites of Ottawa.

This map is not in scale and it doesn't include all of the buildings in downtown Ottawa or Gatineau.

Tour Instructions

1. Leave the Chateau Laurier hotel (D5) and turn west on Wellington Street. As you cross the bridge, look north. On what canal is this set of locks?

2. Walk west to Parliament Hill. It is in grid square D4. The Flame in front of the Parliament Building was lit in 1967 to celebrate Canada's 100th birthday. How old is Canada today?

3. You can tour the Centre Block on Parliament Hill to visit the Library. This is the only part of the building that survived a fire in 1916. What can you climb to see a view of the city?

4. Go back to Wellington Street and walk to D3. There you can tour Canada's highest court of law. You must be very quiet. The judges are making decisions that will affect all Canadians. What is this building called?

5. Hop on the bus and cross the Pont du Portage. As you cross, look west. What body of water can you see in the background?

6. The bus drops you off in block C3. What city and province are you in now? What is the name of the museum there?

7. Cross the bridge east of the museum. This will bring you back to Ottawa. Go to the building made of steel and glass in C4. You will see many types of visual art. What is the name of this building?

8. In grid square C5, you will find a museum that displays the money used in Canada. What is the name of this museum?

9. Another museum near it displays uniforms and weapons used by soldiers who fought in wars around the world. What is the museum's name?

10. Walk to the market in D5. It is famous for a delicious treat called Beaver Tails. These are pastries shaped like a beaver tail. They are topped with sugar and cinnamon, or just about anything you like!

Go to www.duvaleducation.com/ourcountrycanada2. Click on the link to Canada to learn more about Ottawa.

Learning About Provinces and Territories

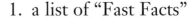

Share the task of learning about the thirteen different provinces and territories! This is an opportunity for you to help others learn and have others help you.

Your teacher has already set up groups for working together on provinces and territories. Each group will present information to the rest of the class about one province or territory.

The maps inside the front and back covers of the textbook provide useful information about Canada.

Everyone will be expected to ask questions and discuss each presentation with the group doing it. You will also need to put information about each presentation in your notebook.

Each presenting group will give you a province/territory fact sheet.

The materials that your group makes for this presentation will be part of your final Canada Project. Include all five of the following parts in your presentation.

1. a list of "Fast Facts"
   - name of province/territory
   - capital city
   - land area
   - official symbols
   - population
   - major imports and exports
   - special features such as "the biggest…" or "the tallest…"

2. a description of the physical features, climate, vegetation, animals, and natural resources
   - Identify each physical region and explain where it is found in your province/territory.
   - Choose an interesting form for this part; for example, a news report, a booklet or pamphlet, a scroll, a photo essay, a series of drawings with captions.

3. copies of notes to hand out to your audience (summarize the facts in numbers 1 and 2)

4. a map with boundaries, major landforms and bodies of water, important places, capital city, and natural resources
   - Include all of the correct parts of a map.

5. a creative form showing or telling about something special in your province/territory
   - for example, a poem and picture, a story, a model or sculpture, a painting, a slideshow, a play, or a poster

British Columbia

Fast Facts

- 924 815 square km of land
- Population 4 113 487
- Cordillera and Interior Plains regions

Nickname: Beautiful BC

Capital: Victoria

Exports: electricity, lumber, fruits and vegetables, fish, metal products, minerals, flowers

Imports: petroleum products, fuel, meat and food products, equipment, chemicals, pharmaceuticals, electricity

Environment

- rocky islands, high mountains, deep inlets on Pacific coast
- climate varies from mild and damp to desert-like
- some of world's largest trees in Pacific Rim National Park
- three mountain ranges, fast rivers, and deep valleys affect transportation routes
- small amount of agricultural land in valleys and on plateaus

Natural Resources

- salmon, herring, cod, oysters, and halibut in the ocean
- coal, oil, and natural gas
- gold, copper, zinc, and silver
- forests cover more than half the province

Industries and Products

- industries: forestry, tourism, mining, agriculture, fishing, manufacturing
- major hydroelectric dams on the Peace and Columbia Rivers
- fruit grown in Okanagan Valley
- vegetables, berries, fruits, flowers, and dairy products from Lower Fraser Valley
- beef cattle raised on grasslands on the interior plateau
- manufacturing includes wood and paper products, food, machinery, computers, electronic equipment

People and Places

- Vancouver, the largest city, is at the mouth of the Fraser River. It is the third-largest city in Canada.
- Victoria, the provincial capital, is on Vancouver Island.

Something Special

- Butchart Gardens in Victoria
- Capilano Suspension Bridge
- totem poles and West Coast First Nations art
- BC is host to the 2010 Winter Olympic and Paralympic Games in Vancouver and Whistler.

Website

Go to www.duvaleducation.com/ourcountrycanada2. Click on the link to learn more about British Columbia.

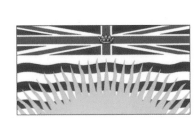

Pacific Dogwood

Steller's Jay

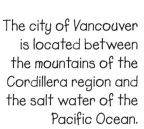

The city of Vancouver is located between the mountains of the Cordillera region and the salt water of the Pacific Ocean.

Fireweed

Common Raven

Yukon

Fast Facts

- 474 711 square km of land
- Population 30 372
- Cordillera, Arctic Lowlands, and Interior Plains regions

Nickname: North of 60

Capital: Whitehorse

Exports: gold and other minerals, natural gas

Imports: machinery, oil, manufactured goods, fresh food and dairy products

Environment

- north of 60° N latitude, partly within the Arctic Circle
- mostly in the Cordillera region; small area on the north coast in the Arctic Lowlands region
- long, cold winters and permafrost; few roads
- several huge glaciers and the largest non-polar icefield in the world
- Aurora Borealis (Northern Lights)
- large numbers of animals: wood bison and muskoxen; last remaining large herd of barren ground caribou; moose, mountain sheep, deer, timber wolves, black and brown bears, grizzly bears

- summer breeding grounds of geese, swans, ducks, and numerous shorebirds; ptarmigan remain all year
- Arctic grayling, northern pike, rainbow and lake trout, whitefish, and salmon

Natural Resources

- lead, zinc, gold, silver, copper, coal, and natural gas

Industries and Products

- most important industries are mining and tourism
- fur trade remains important
- small fishing industry

People and Places

- Whitehorse is the territorial capital of the Yukon. It is also the regional headquarters for the Royal Canadian Mounted Police. It is on a major transportation route linking Canada and Alaska. Two-thirds of the population of the Yukon live in Whitehorse.

Something Special

- Klondike Gold Rush took place here over 100 years ago
- Every year, teams compete in the Yukon Quest, a 1600 km sled dog race that takes up to two weeks to complete!

Website

Go to www.duvaleducation.com/ ourcountrycanada2. Click on the link to learn more about the Yukon.

At 5959 metres, Mount Logan in Kluane National Park is the highest point in Canada.

Alberta

Fast Facts

- 640 045 square km of land
- Population 3 290 350
- Interior Plains, Cordillera, and Canadian Shield regions

Nickname: Sunny Alberta

Capital: Edmonton

Exports: oil and natural gas, beef and other meat products, wheat, chemicals, telephones, lumber products

Imports: automobiles, food products, cattle, manufactured goods, seafood, farm machinery, pharmaceuticals, computers

Environment

- wide variety of landforms: mountains, foothills, plains, and badlands. Many fossils of dinosaurs have been found in the badlands.
- Rocky Mountains and foothills along western border
- Cypress Hills in southeastern Alberta have unique types of vegetation

Natural Resources

- large amount of land suitable for farming or ranching
- largest deposits of oil and natural gas in Canada
- coal, forests, hydroelectricity

Industries and Products

- oil and gas industry most important source of income and employment
- agriculture, especially grains and beef
- plastics and other products made from oil
- forestry, tourism

People and Places

- Edmonton is the provincial capital. It is a centre for grain shipping and meat processing and has many oil refineries. It is Canada's sixth-largest city.
- Calgary, in southern Alberta, has main offices of many oil and gas companies. It is Canada's fifth-largest city.
- Calgary hosted the Winter Olympics in 1988.
- Banff, in the Rocky Mountains, was Canada's first national park. Visitors come to see the natural wonders and many types of wildlife.

Something Special

- an NHL-size skating rink and a huge pool with its own beach and waves at West Edmonton Mall
- chuckwagon races at the Calgary Stampede
- Dinosaur Provincial Park became a UNESCO World Heritage Site in 1979 because of its fossils.

Website

Go to www.duvaleducation.com/ourcountrycanada2. Click on the link to learn more about Alberta.

Wild Rose

Great Horned Owl

In the Alberta badlands, hoodoos were formed by erosion where a layer of harder rock sits on top of softer rock.

Mountain Avens

Gyrfalcon

Northwest Territories

Fast Facts

- 1 140 835 square km of land
- Population 41 464
- Cordillera, Interior Plains, Arctic Lowlands and Canadian Shield regions

Nickname: Land of the Midnight Sun

Capital: Yellowknife

Exports: oil and natural gas, metals, diamonds, artworks

Imports: fresh foods and dairy products, manufactured products, machinery and equipment

Environment

- north of 60° N
- huge land of mountains, forests, tundra, clean rivers, and thousands of clear lakes
- sun never sets at mid-summer; never rises at mid-winter
- Aurora Borealis (Northern Lights)
- animal life includes Arctic foxes, beluga whales, several kinds of bears, moose, and herds of bison and caribou

Natural Resources

- gold, silver, diamonds, uranium, copper, lead, zinc
- oil and natural gas in Beaufort Sea; coal in Mackenzie Valley
- Mackenzie River is the longest in Canada

Industries and Products

- mining, oil and gas, tourism
- one of the world's top three producers of diamonds
- fur trapping, fishing, and hunting remain important
- commercial fishing for whitefish, pickerel, Arctic char
- arts and crafts

People and Places

- a small population in a large land area: most communities located along rivers and large lakes, and along the Arctic coast
- about half the population is Aboriginal
- Yellowknife is the capital of the Northwest Territories. It is a centre for business, transportation, and government services. The Mackenzie Highway connects Yellowknife with Edmonton, almost 1000 km south.

Something Special

- Many Aboriginal people here live traditional lifestyles, gathering food from the land, but even in small communities "out on the land," satellite television and the Internet connect people to the rest of the world.
- eleven official languages

Website

Go to www.duvaleducation.com/ourcountrycanada2. Click on the link to learn more about the Northwest Territories.

Transportation by air is often the only option in the Northwest Territories.

Saskatchewan

Fast Facts

- 588 276 square km of land
- Population 968 157
- Interior Plains and Canadian Shield regions

Nickname: Land of the Living Skies

Capital: Regina

Exports: oil and natural gas, livestock, wood, pulp and paper products, uranium, wheat, canola, barley, farm equipment, steel products, fertilizer

Imports: farm machinery, computers, petroleum products, electricity, seafood

Environment

- a vast, flat land in the south; the second-largest plains area
- huge region of Canadian Shield region, with rocks, lakes, and forests
- waterfowl migrate across Saskatchewan in huge numbers each spring and autumn, feeding and resting in wetlands and grain fields
- cold winters, hot summers, low precipitation in plains area; drought and hail can affect crops

Natural Resources

- almost half of Canada's farmland; ideal for growing field crops
- huge amounts of potash and uranium
- salt, copper, zinc, and nickel
- coal, oil, natural gas

Industries and Products

- greatest grower of wheat in North America
- produces about one-fifth of the oil in Canada
- the world's largest potash industry
- manufacturing of food products and farming equipment

People and Places

- Regina is the provincial capital, a centre for transportation by road and rail, and a business and government centre.
- Saskatoon is the largest city. It is a service centre for agriculture, nearby potash mines, and uranium mines in northern Saskatchewan. The South Saskatchewan River divides the city in two. Seven bridges connect the city.

Something Special

- All new members of the Royal Canadian Mounted Police (RCMP) receive their training in Regina. A new RCMP museum opened there in 2007.
- The city of Estevan is known as the sunniest place in Canada. It averages about 2540 hours of sunshine per year.

Website

Go to www.duvaleducation.com/ourcountrycanada2. Click on the link to learn more about Saskatchewan.

Western Red Lily

Sharp-tailed Grouse

Saskatchewan has been called "Canada's Breadbasket."

Prairie Crocus

Great Gray Owl

Manitoba

Fast Facts

- 552 370 square km of land
- Population 1 148 401
- Interior Plains, Canadian Shield, and Hudson Bay Lowlands regions

Nickname: The Keystone Province

Capital: Winnipeg

Exports: agricultural products, electricity, machinery and equipment, metal products, frozen potatoes, sunflower seeds

Imports: manufactured goods, seafood products

Environment

- one of the sunniest provinces in Canada
- lies in the geographic centre of Canada
- southern Manitoba is flat, low-lying plains; most central and northern parts are in the Canadian Shield region
- also part of the Hudson Bay Lowlands region, with wetlands and some coniferous forest
- tundra in the extreme north: stunted trees, exposed rock, and swamps
- lakes and large rivers cover about one-sixth of Manitoba
- Lake Winnipeg is Canada's fifth-largest lake

Natural Resources

- nickel, gold, silver, copper, zinc, and lead
- good agricultural land

Industries and Products

- large hydroelectric power plants on the Nelson River
- wheat, canola, and flaxseed
- other crops include buckwheat, peas, sunflowers, sugar beets, oats, and barley
- beef cattle, hogs, and poultry
- only tantalum mine in North America at Bernic Lake. Tantalum is used to make electronics, cell phones, aircraft controls, and missile parts.
- manufacturing of food products and farm machinery

People and Places

- Winnipeg is the provincial capital. More than half the people in the province live there. The Royal Winnipeg Ballet is a well-known dance company that tours across Canada and elsewhere.
- Portage la Prairie is a smaller city in the heart of the grain-growing belt. It has a museum containing a replica of Fort la Reine, the fort built by Pierre Gaultier de La Vérendrye when he explored the region in the 1700s.

Something Special

- A branch of the Royal Canadian Mint is located in Winnipeg. All Canadian coins are made there.
- Visitors from all over the world come to Churchill to visit the world's largest denning area for polar bears.

Website

Go to www.duvaleducation.com/ourcountrycanada2. Click on the link to learn more about Manitoba.

Most sunflower seeds are used to produce cooking oil.

Nunavut

Fast Facts

- 1 932 255 square km of land
- Population 29 474
- Arctic Lowlands and Canadian Shield regions

Nunavut means "our land" in Inuktitut, the Inuit language

Capital: Iqaluit

Exports: diamonds, fish, artworks

Imports: electricity, airplane parts, fresh food and dairy products, machinery, manufactured goods

Environment

- includes several of Canada's largest islands, including the biggest: Baffin Island
- two-thirds of Canada's coastline
- less precipitation in northern area than certain areas of the Sahara Desert
- water frozen much of the year, so plants unable to use it; plants grow very slowly and do not get large
- tundra and barren lands, with plants far apart and rocky earth exposed

Natural Resources

- diamonds, copper, gold, silver, lead, zinc
- oil, coal, and natural gas

Industries and Products

- mining, tourism
- arts and crafts
- no agricultural land and very short growing season; hunting and fishing important for obtaining food

People and Places

- Nunavut became Canada's third territory in 1999.
- 85% of the people are Inuit; Inuktitut is one of four official languages
- just 28 permanent communities and only one inland: Baker Lake
- Iqaluit is the territorial capital and the largest community; a centre of government, transportation, and business.

Something Special

- Almost every community has an airport or airstrip.
- There are more snowmobiles than cars; airplanes are used to transport people, food, machinery, and anything else needed in outlying areas.

Website

Go to www.duvaleducation.com/ourcountrycanada2. Click on the link to learn more about Nunavut.

Purple Saxifrage

Rock Ptarmigan

Nunavut is Canada's largest territory and has the youngest population overall.

White Trillium

Common Loon

The St. Lawrence–Great Lakes Seaway is a navigable waterway 3790 km long.

Ontario

Fast Facts

- 907 574 square km of land
- Population 12 160 282
- Canadian Shield, Hudson Bay Lowlands, and St. Lawrence Lowlands regions

Nickname: The Heartland of Canada

Capital: Toronto

Exports: cars, trucks, and vehicle parts, electricity, machinery and equipment, electronics products, fruit, vegetables, food products, chemicals

Imports: oil and natural gas, electricity, food and dairy products, seafood, wood and paper products

Environment

- rocks, lakes, rivers, and forests of the Canadian Shield region cover about half of Ontario
- wetlands and coniferous forests of Hudson Bay Lowlands region are flat and poorly drained, but provide a home for many animals and birds
- many major river systems
- St. Lawrence Lowlands region has deep fertile soil, mild climate
- Niagara Escarpment is a limestone ridge running 725 km from Queenston to Manitoulin Island

Natural Resources

- iron, copper, lead, nickel, zinc, gold, silver, and uranium in Canadian Shield region
- petroleum: oil and natural gas found in southwestern Ontario

- forests
  - softwood trees from coniferous forests for pulp and paper
  - deciduous hardwood trees harvested in some areas for building and furniture manufacturing
  - government of Ontario owns over 90% of Ontario's forest lands, issues special timber licences to logging companies to harvest trees. Government laws also protect forests because they are valuable for recreation and tourism.
- water
  - many rivers and lakes provide transportation, hydroelectric power, and recreational space
  - the five Great Lakes together contain one-fifth of the world's fresh water
  - St. Lawrence Seaway connects the St. Lawrence River system to the Great Lakes. This waterway is the cheapest way to transport bulky items such as grain, minerals, and newsprint.
  - fast-moving rivers and streams are an excellent source of hydroelectric power used by homes and industries
  - 400 000 lakes and rivers
- fertile soil: the St. Lawrence Lowlands region contains some of Ontario's largest cities as well as fruit, grain, dairy, and mixed farms.

Industries and Products

- manufacturing, mining, tourism, forestry, financial services
- Ontario is the leading manufacturing province in Canada. Products include food, machinery, chemicals, and electronic products.
- agricultural products, including cattle feed, dairy products, meat, vegetables, fruit
- nickel, uranium, copper, gold, zinc, and iron mined and exported
- forestry products, including pulp, paper, and lumber
- Ontario produces electricity from water, coal, oil, and nuclear generators. However, it uses more than it produces, so it also must import electricity.
- Financial services and banking are a major industry.

People and Places

- Ontario is the second-largest province in Canada. It has more than one-third of Canada's population.
- Most of Ontario's population, agriculture, and industry are found in the smallest physical region. About 90% of the people live in the province's St. Lawrence Lowlands area.
- Ottawa is the national capital.
- Toronto is the largest city in Canada. In 1998, six boroughs joined together to become a "megacity." There are about 5.4 million people in the Greater Toronto Area.
- Toronto is the provincial capital. It is a centre for business, banking, industry, transportation, and technology.

Rail lines cross hundreds of kilometres of the Canadian Shield region to connect Central Canada with Western Canada.

- Many cites in the southeastern area have large manufacturing industries producing products for sale outside the region.
- Other Ontario cities, such as Sault Ste. Marie and Thunder Bay, are mainly involved in transportation and providing services to mining, forestry, and people living in the surrounding areas.

Something Special

- The main downtown road in Toronto is Yonge Street. This is the longest street in the world.

Website

Go to www.duvaleducation.com/ourcountrycanada2. Click on the link to learn more about Ontario.

Toronto, Ontario, can be easily recognized by the CN Tower, one of the world's largest free-standing structures.

Map Reading: Boundaries

Boundaries are imaginary lines on a globe, road map, or atlas. They are used to outline the outside edges of a political region. When they separate two countries, they are called international boundaries. These are also called borders.

Boundaries also separate political regions within a country. In Canada, these are called provincial and territorial boundaries. They show where one province or territory ends and another begins.

The province of Ontario is divided into districts in the north and counties in the south. Municipal boundaries outline areas that have a local government, such as cities, towns, and villages.

Detailed maps may show villages, towns, and cities. The size of the place is shown by the symbol used. The legend of the map will show you what the symbols stand for.

Southeastern Ontario

Do ◆ Discuss ◆ Discover

1. Examine the map on this page very carefully.

   a) Identify the symbols used for international, provincial, and county boundaries. Name examples in your notebook.

   b) Identify the symbols and find examples of a village, a town, and a city.

Québec

Fast Facts

- 1 356 367 square km of land
- Population 7 546 131
- Canadian Shield, Hudson Bay Lowlands, St. Lawrence Lowlands, and Appalachian regions

Nickname: *La belle province* (The Beautiful Province)

Capital: Québec

Exports: electricity, pharmaceutical products, aluminum, knitted products, clothing and textiles, maple syrup

Imports: food products, automobiles, vehicle parts, electricity, lumber, metal products

Environment

- the largest province in Canada; almost entirely surrounded by water
- more than one million lakes and rivers
- polar bears and caribou live in the northern part

Natural Resources

- asbestos, gold, iron, copper, silver, zinc, lead, and other minerals
- one of the largest forested areas in Canada
- St. Lawrence River is one of the world's largest rivers

Industries and Products

- farming, industry, and business centred along the St. Lawrence River
- many of Canada's manufactured products are made in Québec
- clothing and fabrics, food, paper, metal and wood products, machinery, electronics, aircraft
- pulp and paper produced from the forests
- hydroelectricity produced along the St. Lawrence, Saguenay, St. Maurice Rivers and La Grande Rivière
- electricity exported to Ontario, New Brunswick, and northeastern United States

People and Places

- Most people speak French as their first language.
- Most of the population lives in the St. Lawrence Lowlands region; most of Québec's largest cities are also located there.
- Montréal is the largest city. Many companies have their headquarters or head offices situated there. It is an important business and cultural centre. Montréal was the home of Expo 67 and the 1976 Summer Olympics.
- The city of Québec is the provincial capital. It is a historic and beautiful city. It is the seventh-largest city in Canada.

White Garden Lily

Snowy Owl

Something Special

- The city of Québec is one of Canada's oldest cities and was the first city in North America to be chosen as a World Heritage Site.

Website

Go to www.duvaleducation.com/ourcountrycanada2. Click on the link to learn more about Québec.

Two features of the Québec Winter Carnival are Bonhomme and an ice sculpture competition.

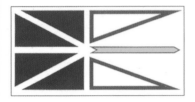

Pitcher Plant

Atlantic Puffin

Newfoundland and Labrador

Fast Facts

- 370 495 square km of land
- Population 505 469
- Canadian Shield, St. Lawrence Lowlands, and Appalachian regions

Nickname: The Rock

Capital: St. John's

Exports: oil, fish and seafood products, electricity, metal ore

Imports: fresh food and dairy products, oil, machinery, equipment

Environment

- the most easterly province in Canada
- two parts: Labrador on the mainland and the island of Newfoundland
- rocky cliffs, mountain ranges, lakes, and rivers; 17 000 km of rugged coastline
- most of Labrador is in the Canadian Shield region (A small part of the south coast is part of the St. Lawrence Lowlands region.)
- island of Newfoundland is part of the Appalachian region
- continental shelf and Grand Banks off the shore of Newfoundland
- in Labrador, vegetation either coniferous forest or tundra
- sea ice and icebergs move down the coast in the ocean currents
- Labrador's winter climate is cold and storms are frequent

Natural Resources

- Grand Banks, one of the most important fisheries in the world; restrictions on fishing today because few fish remain
- gold, iron, nickel, copper, lead, zinc, and asbestos

Industries and Products

- mining, fisheries, newsprint, oil and natural gas, tourism
- offshore petroleum produced at the Hibernia oil field on the Grand Banks
- uranium mined in Labrador and nickel at Voisey Bay
- hydroelectricity produced at Churchill Falls, Labrador
- newsprint at three pulp and paper mills

People and Places

- the last area to become a province of Canada, in 1949
- St. John's is the provincial capital. It is a port city located near the main shipping lanes of the North Atlantic Ocean and near the Hibernia offshore oil fields. It is one of North America's oldest cities.

Something Special

- In 1901, Guglielmo Marconi, an inventor, received the first wireless message across the Atlantic at Cabot Tower.

Website

Go to www.duvaleducation.com/ ourcountrycanada2. Click on the link to learn more about Newfoundland and Labrador.

Cabot Tower on Signal Hill is named after explorer John Cabot, who arrived in Newfoundland more than 400 years ago.

New Brunswick

Fast Facts

- 71 355 square km of land
- Population 729 997
- Appalachian region

Nickname: The Picture Province

Capital: Fredericton

Exports: petroleum products, coal, meat, fish, dairy products, fruit, vegetables, lumber and wood products

Imports: oil, food products, chemicals, pharmaceutical products

Environment

- Gulf of St. Lawrence lies along the eastern coast; the Bay of Fundy lies between New Brunswick and Nova Scotia
- several important rivers; the longest is the Saint John River
- tides and ocean currents create unusual shoreline landforms and the warmest beaches in the Maritimes
- highest tides in the world occur in the Bay of Fundy

Natural Resources

- silver, zinc, lead, gold, copper, potash, antimony
- forests cover over 80% of the province
- coal, oil, natural gas, peat

Industries and Products

- mining, forestry, agriculture, fishing, tourism
- manufacturing of food, wood products, paper, textiles, and transportation equipment
- salmon, trout, oysters, and mussels raised by aquaculture
- information technology, with many call centres

People and Places

- One-third of the population is francophone, which means they are French-speaking or have French ancestors.
- Moncton is nicknamed the Hub of the Maritimes because many transportation routes in the Maritime provinces pass through it.
- Fredericton, located on the Saint John River, is the provincial capital. It is a centre of government and education.
- Fredericton is home to a college that trains forest rangers.
- Canada's largest oil refinery is in Saint John.

Something Special

- Canada's only officially bilingual province
- The Reversing Falls on the Bay of Fundy is one of the marine wonders of the world; the tides push their way against the river current and actually reverse the flow of the rapids. The river runs backwards!

Website

Go to www.duvaleducation.com/ourcountrycanada2. Click on the link to learn more about New Brunswick.

Purple Violet

Black-capped Chickadee

The Flowerpot Rocks at Hopewell Cape were created by the action of the ocean.

Mayflower

Osprey

Nova Scotia

Fast Facts

- 52 917 square km of land
- Population 913 462
- Appalachian region

Nickname: Canada's Ocean Playground

Capital: Halifax

Exports: natural gas, tires, food and dairy products, fruit, lumber, fish and shellfish

Imports: vehicle parts, machinery, manufactured products

Environment

- almost an island, but joined to New Brunswick by a narrow piece of land
- jagged coastline, with nearly 4000 rocky outcroppings and islands
- Cape Breton Island connected to the rest of Nova Scotia by the Canso Causeway
- visited by many migrating birds every year
- whales found off the coast where fish and seafood are plentiful

Natural Resources

- forests, many lakes and streams
- coal, gypsum, peat, salt, offshore oil and gas
- the second-largest natural harbour in the world at Halifax; deep water keeps it ice-free

Industries and Products

- fishing, forestry, mining, agriculture, tourism
- shellfish harvesting (lobster, crab, shrimp)
- aquaculture produces salmon, halibut, clams, and oysters
- softwood and hardwood lumber, pulp and paper
- coal mining; coal used in generators to provide most of the province's power
- Annapolis Tidal Generating Station uses tides to make electricity; the first tidal hydroelectric plant in Canada
- offshore natural gas fields near Sable Island
- types of farms include dairy, poultry, and fruit (apples, blueberries, grapes)
- manufacturing of railway freight cars

People and Places

- Most people live along the coast, with about half of them in small towns and small seaports in sheltered coves and bays.
- Halifax is the provincial capital. It is a historic port city with a busy international shipping industry.

Something Special

- The tides in the Bay of Fundy rise higher than a four-storey building, up to 15 metres. In the historic village of Bear River, all the buildings are on stilts.

Website

Go to www.duvaleducation.com/ourcountrycanada2. Click on the link to learn more about Nova Scotia.

The town of Lunenberg is a World Heritage Site for its historic character. The famous *Bluenose* sailing ship, which you can see on the back of a dime, was built here.

Prince Edward Island

Fast Facts

- 5684 square km of land
- Population 135 851
- Appalachian region

Nickname: Garden of the Gulf

Capital: Charlottetown

Exports: potatoes (fresh and frozen), fish and seafood, food products, Irish moss (seaweed)

Imports: petroleum, transportation equipment, manufactured products, electricity

Environment

- the smallest province of Canada, about 230 km long and from 6 to 60 km wide
- almost no inland bodies of fresh water
- highest point on the island, at Springton, only 52 m above sea level
- fine white beaches on the northern side of the island
- low outcroppings of red sandstone about 6 m high border the southern side

Natural Resources

- fish, lobsters, and shellfish
- good soils and mild climate the basis of the farming industry

Industries and Products

- agriculture, tourism, fishing
- the top producer of potatoes in Canada
- no extensive original forests, but trees grown in woodlots for fuel and some lumber
- Irish moss, used to make ice cream, harvested on horseback
- no hydroelectric power; most electricity imported from Nova Scotia by undersea cable

- three wind farms plus a hydrogen-fuel station part of a plan to develop alternative energy sources

People and Places

- Charlottetown is the provincial capital city and the Island's largest city. The Charlottetown Conference in 1864 set the stage for the formation of Canada as a nation. Charlottetown is called the "Birthplace of Confederation."

Something Special

- Confederation Centre of the Arts has several theatres, an art gallery, and a library. It is the site of the Charlottetown Festival. Each year, it produces a musical, *Anne of Green Gables*, based on the novel by local author Lucy Maud Montgomery.

Lady's Slipper

Website

Go to www.duvaleducation.com/ourcountrycanada2. Click on the link to learn more about Prince Edward Island.

Blue Jay

When you see reddish coloured rock or soil, there are traces of iron present. It turns the soil the colour of rusty iron.

With half its land under cultivation, Prince Edward Island is known as the Garden of the Gulf.

Chapter 9

Knowledge and Understanding

1. Following the presentations on the provinces and territories, work with a partner to develop a comparison chart for any two provinces or territories. (Hints: Compare the province/territory you are focusing on in the Canada Project with one other province/territory. See page 12 for examples of comparison charts.)

2. Identify vocabulary from this chapter to add to the vocabulary section of your notebook. Draw diagrams or sketches to help you remember the words and their meanings.

3. Create an organizer that matches every province and territory to its region(s).

Inquiry/Research and Communication Skills

4. Draw a poster to encourage visitors to a point of interest in either Ottawa or any one of the provinces or territories. Include a picture, a slogan, an address, and prices if needed.

Map, Globe, and Graphic Skills

5. a) Use an atlas and what you have learned about grids to locate the latitude and longitude for your hometown or city. Put this into your notebook.

   b) Locate and label your hometown or city on the outline map of Canada in your notes.

Application

6. Imagine you are visiting Ottawa for one day. Write an illustrated story or journal about your day.

7. In a small group, use the Ottawa tour map to create new scavenger questions for another group. Use the grid clues to help you form proper clues.

The Canada Project

1. Research and create a fact card (like a baseball card) for the capital city and one other city in your province/territory. Remember to put a picture on the front.

The Canada Project

It is now time for all groups to work on the relief model of Canada. Follow the steps below to build the display.

Step 1:

- In your small group, create an outline of your province/ territory on heavy white cardboard. Use an overhead projector to enlarge and trace your part of a map of Canada. Each group needs to use the same base map. That way, all of the provinces and territories will have the same scale and Canada will fit together!

- Use a pencil to sketch the major waterways, landforms, and cities onto your map. Look at the relief map on page 7 (or in your atlas) to figure out the position and elevations of landforms. Your pencil sketch and this information will help at the next stage.

- Carefully cut out the outline of your province/territory.

Step 2:

- As a class, create a continuous sheet of recycled flattened cardboard boxes. You will use it as a base for the final relief model map. Tape the edges of the boxes together and reinforce the joints or seams with extra tape.

- Place your province/territory on the cardboard sheet. (Don't attach it.) Consult with your neighbouring provinces/territories to check that rivers and other features that cross boundaries are correct. Make corrections to your pencil sketch and notes.

> **Coming Up**
> Do not glue your province/territory to the cardboard backing yet. You will add more information as you complete the Canada Project.

Step 3:

- Use modelling dough or clay to create a relief map of your province/territory. Add landforms and bodies of water based on your notes and sketches. Consult with your neighbouring provinces/ territories about the elevation of features that cross boundaries. You want the landscape to be continuous.

- Let your relief map dry and then paint it.

- Add labels for landforms, bodies of water, capital cities, and other important places.

Chapter 10
Connections

Transportation

Services

Connections

Resources and Products

Information and Ideas

We have learned that Canada is a large country with many natural differences. Travel and communication are important to Canadians. They connect across the country with each other every day in hundreds of ways.

Focus on Learning

In this chapter, you will learn about
- transportation
- writing a paragraph
- resources and products
- interviewing
- information and ideas
- services

Vocabulary

transportation	services
economy	public
communication	transportation
innovation	

Transportation

Transportation refers to methods of moving people and goods from one place to another.

Canada has more than 900 000 kilometres of public roads and more than 72 000 kilometres of railroad tracks. It has about 1149 airports. Of these, 26 major airports handle 94% of all airline passengers. There are about 120 ferry services that carry passengers, automobiles, and freight across bodies of water.

Transportation is one of the most important ways Canadians are connected. People and goods are constantly on the move.

Trans means "across." Port is the root of a word that means "to carry."

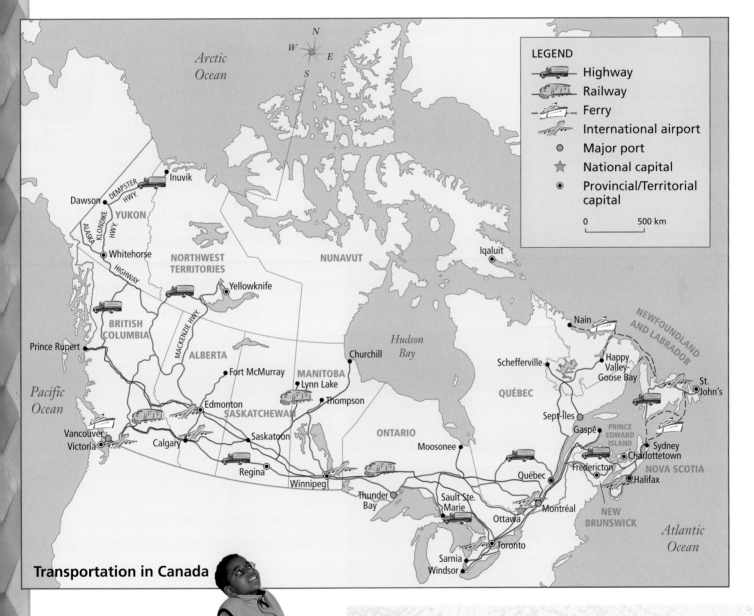

Transportation in Canada

Do ◆ Discuss ◆ Discover

1. On an outline map of Canada, show routes that each of the seven students may have used to get to Ottawa from the different regions of Canada. Use a different colour for each. Put the map into your notebook.

On the Move

Canadians use many different means of moving people and products. The choice of method is affected by the size and weight of the load, distance to be travelled, barriers to travel, and the speed required.

Other Ways of Moving Things

Information and energy are also carried or sent to others across the country and around the world. Some methods used are

- fibre optics
- satellites
- radio waves
- telephone lines
- power lines
- pipelines

Do ◆ Discuss ◆ Discover

1. a) Review pages 127 and 128 and work in small groups to brainstorm examples of land, water, and air transportation. Give two examples of materials or products that could be transported by each method.

   b) As a class, share your ideas and create a master list of the types of transportation on chart paper. Post it on the wall in your classroom.

Writing a Paragraph

Good paragraphs have three parts:

1. The first sentence tells what the paragraph will be about.

2. The sentences in the middle give more information about the topic.

3. The last sentence finishes the paragraph with an interesting comment about the topic.

There are three steps to writing a paragraph:

Step 1: Develop an idea about the topic. One good way is to create a web of facts you know about the topic. Here is an example:

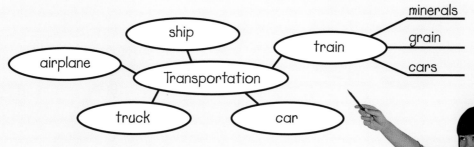

Step 2: Plan your paragraph using the information from the idea web.

- What will you say about the topic in your opening sentence?

- What will you say about each supporting idea in the middle sentences?

- What is the best order to put them in?

- What will your closing sentence say about the topic?

Step 3: Use the plan to write your paragraph.

Reread your paragraph and correct any errors. Write out your final, finished copy.

Do ◆ Discuss ◆ Discover

Choose either question 1 or 2:

1. Look back at the map you did on page 127. Choose one of the seven students who came to Ottawa. Write a paragraph about his or her journey to Ottawa for the conference. What forms of transportation did they use? In what sequence did they use them?

2. Write a paragraph about a trip you have taken and the forms of transportation you used. Describe where you went and include something interesting and fun that you did.

How Does It Get There?

Canada is a country rich with raw materials. Manufacturing industries turn these raw materials into products that make everyday life more comfortable. Follow iron ore as it travels around Ontario and is made into a car.

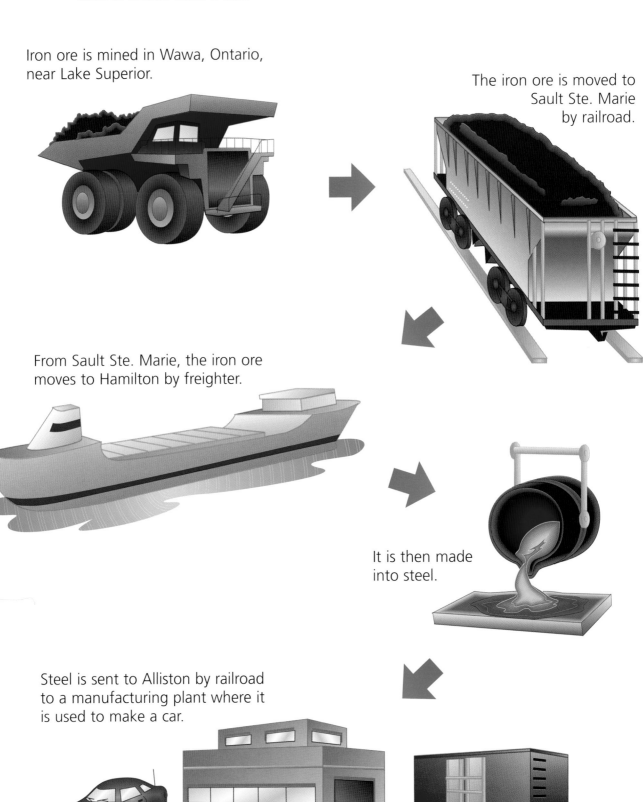

Iron ore is mined in Wawa, Ontario, near Lake Superior.

The iron ore is moved to Sault Ste. Marie by railroad.

From Sault Ste. Marie, the iron ore moves to Hamilton by freighter.

It is then made into steel.

Steel is sent to Alliston by railroad to a manufacturing plant where it is used to make a car.

Resources and Products

Manufacturing industries turn raw materials into products. Some industries process or refine raw materials. This means they change them into a different, more useful state. For example, a smelter processes raw iron ore into pure iron.

Other industries turn processed materials into final products. For example, cars are manufactured from many different parts. Metal, plastic, rubber, glass, and other types of parts are assembled into a final product.

In the photos on this page, workers are involved in the food industry, the clothing industry, the auto industry, and the construction industry.

The provinces and territories of Canada buy and sell resources and products to and from each other and places outside Canada. The **economy** is based on exchange.

If a place has many resources or if it manufactures many products that other places wish to buy, it will have a strong economy.

Do ◆ Discuss ◆ Discover

1. In groups of three, brainstorm examples of industries. Think of as many ideas as you can. Share your ideas with another group and make any changes or corrections necessary. Put these lists into your notebook.

Shopping Day

Food Products

Breakfast CEREAL

MILK

GRAPE JUICE

MAPLE SYRUP

LEAN Steak

Other Products

Daily News
This Just In!

Motor Oil

Plastic Garbage Bags

Peat Moss

1¢ $1 25¢
$2 5¢ 1¢ 10¢
10¢ 1¢
10¢ 25 5¢ 1¢

Do ◆ Discuss ◆ Discover

1. In groups of three, choose four products from the items above. Discuss the following questions. Write out your notes and put them into your notebook.

a) Discuss where in Canada the products on this page might have come from. Remember that some products have several different parts. Where would the different parts have come from?

b) Discuss what kind of packaging each of the items would have. Where did the packaging come from?

c) Energy was used to make and transport all of these products. What types of energy might have been used? Where might it have come from?

Interviewing

An interview is a conversation conducted to gather information. The information may be written down or recorded with the person's permission. Use the following as a guide for interviewing:

- Consider your topic and think of questions for which you would like answers. Key questions for gaining information often begin with who, what, where, when, how, and why.
- You are the interviewer. Pick a person who has information that you would like to learn. This is your interviewee. If you do not know much about the person or the topic, do background research before you begin.
- Write the questions you are going to ask on a piece of paper. Leave lots of space between questions to write down the answers in point form.
- Work with a parent or teacher to arrange a time and a place for the interview. Explain the purpose of the interview to the interviewee. You may want to record the interview as well as take notes by hand. Ask permission if you are going to record.
- Record the interviewee's answers. If a person gives an incomplete answer, always ask a follow-up question so you get the information you need.
- At the end of the session, thank the person. Immediately write out your notes of the answers before you forget what you were told.
- Write up the interview using a format like this:
  Interviewer: "Do you like what you do?"
  Interviewee: "Yes, but it is hard work with long hours."
- Give a copy of the interview to the interviewee. People like to read their answers to your questions. This also gives them a chance to correct any errors in your notes or give you more information.

Information and Ideas

Canadians are connected by the ways they exchange information and ideas with others. This is called **communication**.

There are many ways to communicate ideas and connect with other people.

Radio and television and movies are ways of sharing information, ideas, and entertainment. People hear the voices and see the faces of many Canadians on television.

National newspapers and magazines let people know what is happening all across the country.

Sports teams, such as the Toronto Maple Leafs and the Montréal Canadiens, travel across North America to compete with other teams. People may watch them on television or travel to see them play.

Musicians and songwriters create recordings played by people across Canada. Award-winning Canadian performers such as Nelly Furtado represent Canada to people in other countries.

Many authors have created books that show Canada to others. This house was the setting for *Anne of Green Gables*, by Lucy Maud Montgomery.

Visual artists communicate ideas in paintings, drawings, sculptures, and mixed media objects.

Many special schools, such as Canada's National Ballet School in Toronto, have students from all over the country.

Canadian athletes take part in competitions in Canada and in other countries. Champions such as gold medalist Daniel Igali represent Canada in Olympic Games.

The Internet and e-mail are two ways to share information and ideas with people all over the world.

Do ◆ Discuss ◆ Discover

1. Review the Interviewing section on page 133. Interview one of your parents or another adult.
   - What job do they do?
   - What are two forms of communication they use in their work?
   - Do these forms of communication help make their work easier? If yes, how?
   - What is the main kind of information or ideas they communicate to other Canadians?

   Share the responses with one other student and put the information into your notebook.

2. As a class, create a large group poster called "Communicating in Canada." Each of you will provide one example of an image of a person or event to put on it. Put the poster up in your classroom.

Innovations

An **innovation** is something that is new. Innovations include discovering something that exists but isn't known about, or inventing something new that did not exist before.

Some Canadians are well known because they have invented or discovered something that makes life better for others. Other Canadian inventors are less well known, but their innovations are used and valued by many.

Joseph-Armand Bombardier invented the snowmobile. In northern areas of Canada, the snowmobile has often taken the place of dogsleds.

The discovery of insulin by Sir Frederick Banting and Charles Best has allowed diabetics to live a healthier life.

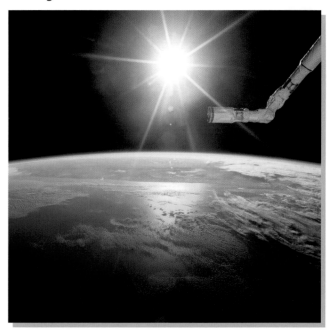

The International Space Station project uses the Canadarm for building and repairing the space station.

James Naismith invented a game for his students using a ball and two peach baskets, which developed into the game of basketball.

Do ◆ Discuss ◆ Discover

1. a) In small groups, discuss why each of the innovations/inventions on this page is important.

   b) Create a chart to show the original problem, the solution provided by the inventor(s), and a few sentences telling how the invention has changed the lives of those who use it. Put this chart into your notebook.

Services

Services are groups or individuals who do something that someone needs. There are many kinds of services. They often supply people with special knowledge, skills, and sometimes equipment.

Not every community can meet the needs of all of the people all of the time. Some services are only needed occasionally. Often, people must come from another community or region to provide the service. This is one way Canadians form connections with each other.

Internet companies and ambulances are examples of service industries.

Most of the banks in Canada have branches all across the country. They assist businesses and individuals with financial help.

People in small, isolated communities may be visited by doctors or nurses at certain regular times. In an emergency, either a doctor flies to see them or they are flown to see the doctor!

The Royal Canadian Mounted Police enforce laws that protect all Canadians. RCMP officers work in all parts of the country.

Industries that are far from cities sometimes need special services. Inspectors travel from one pipeline site to another to check that work is being done safely.

Public transportation includes all of the ways that people pay to ride someplace. People who work on airplanes, buses, trains, and ferries help people get where they are going in Canada.

Many people are employed in tourism, making other people's vacations fun, safe, and comfortable. This visitor is being welcomed by a worker at the Canadian National Exhibition.

Sometimes there is an emergency in a community that affects many people and causes a lot of damage. The Canadian Armed Forces sometimes helps in emergencies and disasters.

Do ◆ Discuss ◆ Discover

1. a) As a class, discuss how people provide services that connect Canadians.
   b) Take a walk through your neighbourhood. Look for information about services to the community. As a class, discuss services in your community. Then write two or three paragraphs about your discussion. Put this into your notebook.

Chapter 10

Knowledge and Understanding

1. Identify vocabulary from this chapter to add to the vocabulary section of your notebook. Draw diagrams or sketches to help you remember the words and their meanings.

2. Identify and list one example of a connection between provinces/territories in the following categories: transportation, resources and products, information and ideas, and services.

3. Explain in point-form notes how the different types of landforms and bodies of water in Canada create challenges for providing services, transporting goods, and communication.

Map, Globe, and Graphic Skills

4. With a partner, sketch a map of your neighbourhood. Label the services (for example, doctor, dentist, post office, bank, hospital, lawyer, plumber, police station). Remember to use symbols, colour, and a legend to show roads and places on the map.

Application

5. In paragraphs, identify and explain how two of the following inventions have made life for people in Canada easier or better.

- snowmobile
- garbage bag
- lacrosse
- snowplow
- telephone
- frozen food
- insulin
- zipper
- basketball
- pacemaker
- light bulb
- electric wheelchair

The Canada Project

In your group, continue the work on the relief model of Canada that you started at the end of Chapter 9.

Step 1:

- In your small group, identify the major natural resources and products produced in your province/territory. Refer to your completed map of Canada you worked on throughout Chapters 2 to 8 for information.

- Make symbols for each natural resource and product. Attach them to your province/ territory model.

Step 2:

- Use a pencil to sketch the major transportation routes (rail, highway, pipelines) in your province/territory. Use the map on page 127 for help. Consult with your neighbouring provinces/territories to make sure the routes cross boundaries correctly. Make corrections to your pencil marks.

- Use different colours of marker pens to carefully mark the pencilled transportation routes in your province/territory. Cooperate with the other students to choose a single system of colours for different types of routes.

The Canada Project – Finishing Touches

The Relief Model

- Work together as each group carefully attaches its province/territory model to the cardboard base to create the relief model of Canada.

- Identify three resources or products that your province/territory exports to another province/territory.

- Use a variety of coloured ribbons or strings to show these exchanges in Canada. Run ribbons or strings from three symbols in your province/territory to provinces/territories that import them. Attach the ribbons or strings onto the relief model using pins or glue.

Focus Questions

- How is your province/territory important to the whole of Canada?

- How is the rest of Canada important to your province/territory?

- What is special about your province/territory?

Let's Meet and Talk About Connections

1. Each group will present its province/territory to the class. Be sure to include the following:

a) Give an interesting and fun introduction to your province/territory. This could be a television commercial, poem, mime, skit, puppet show, or song. Make sure everyone in your group takes part.

b) Present your shoebox and scrapbook. Display the contents of the shoebox. Explain each item. Do the same for the items in the scrapbook. Each person in the group should speak as well as help create the display. Remember to refer to the relief model during your presentation.

2. In Chapters 2 to 8, the seven students each presented a concern in their region, which you have discussed. Each group will now present one of the concerns that is important in its province/territory. If your province/territory is part of more than one region, choose only one of the concerns to present.

a) Consider the following:
   • Clearly identify the concern.
   • Develop a slogan to bring the issue to people's attention.
   • What solutions or actions do you suggest?
   • How can people in other regions help each other?

b) Ask the audience if they have any questions. Answer all the questions as best as you can.

Share the work you have done and enjoy yourselves!

Glossary

A

adaptation—special features of an animal or plant that help it survive; for example, the Arctic hare grows white fur in the winter that makes it difficult for predators to see

animal life—the animals, birds, fish, and other living creatures of an area

aquaculture—the business of raising fish or shellfish as a crop to be harvested; similar to agriculture

Arctic Circle—an imaginary line around the Earth located at 66 ½° N latitude

B

badlands—dry lands where the rocks have been worn into unusual shapes by erosion, as in southeastern Alberta

bar graph—a visual way of showing numerical (number) information; the amounts are shown as bars and measured on a scale marked in units

barren—an area of land with almost no living plants

boundary—a border or a line that outlines a political region such as a country, province, or territory

breed—the act of creating young

C

canal—a narrow channel dug to carry a stream of water; used for transportation or irrigation

capital city—the city where the government of a country, province, or territory meets

cardinal directions—the four main directions on a compass: north, east, south, and west

cartographer—a person who draws maps

chart—an organized way of showing information

climate—the pattern of average temperature and precipitation of a place over a long period of time

communication—exchanging information and ideas with others

comparison chart—an organizer that shows how two or more things are the same and how they are different

compass rose—an illustration on a map that shows the directions

coniferous—trees with needles and cones; sometimes called evergreens

conservation—taking good care of the environment

continental shelf—an area where the ocean floor slants gradually downward for many kilometres and then suddenly drops off into a deep trench

criteria—important characteristics of something, used in making comparisons

D

deciduous—trees that lose their leaves each year and grow new leaves the next season

delta—an area of flat land at the mouth of a river, often shaped like a triangle. Several branches of the river may flow through it to the ocean.

drought—a long time without precipitation

E

economy—the wealth and resources of a place

ecotourism—people travelling to a place to see the animals, vegetation, and landforms in their natural state

elevation—the height of land above or below sea level, usually measured in metres

environment—our surroundings; the air, the land, and the water around us

erosion—natural forces such as wind and water wearing away landforms and carrying the particles away

escarpment—a long rock cliff where the elevation of land changes abruptly

estuary—the wide mouth of a river, where the flow of the river water is affected by ocean tides

F

fertile—the ability of soil to produce healthy plants and crops

G

geographer—a person who studies the surface of the Earth and the effects of human activity on the environment

glacier—a huge mass of ice hundreds of metres deep that grows or shrinks as the climate changes

government—the group of people in a country, province, or city that makes and enforces laws for its citizens

Grand Banks—an area on the continental shelf southeast of Newfoundland and Labrador that is world-famous for fishing

graph—a visual way of organizing and showing numerical (number) information

grid—a pattern of regularly spaced lines forming squares; used to locate information on maps; lines of latitude and longitude

H

habitat—the natural home of an animal or plant

hardwood—lumber made from the hard-to-cut wood of broad-leafed trees such as maple or oak

harvest—the collecting stage of a resource; for example, grain, fish, or lumber

humidity—the amount of water vapour in the air

hydroelectricity—electricity produced by the force of water

I

industry—a business that collects raw materials, creates products for sale, or provides services

innovation—something that is new; a new way of doing something; a discovery or invention of something new

intermediate directions—the directions between the main four directions; for example, northeast

irrigation—a method of bringing water to crops

L

landforms—natural features of the Earth, such as mountains, hills, plateaus, and plains

latitude—imaginary lines that run around the Earth parallel to the equator; used to locate places on the Earth and measure distances north and south of the equator

legend—a list showing the meanings of symbols, colours, and lines used on a map

locks—structures on a waterway used to raise and lower boats in places where the elevation changes greatly

longitude—imaginary lines that reach from the North Pole to the South Pole; used to locate places and time zones on the Earth

M

map—a drawing or diagram of part of the Earth's surface seen from above

meteorite—a rock that comes crashing to Earth from outer space

mouth—(of a river) the place where a river empties into an ocean or large body of water

muskeg—an area of boggy, wet ground and decaying plants

N

natural resources—materials found in nature that are used by people to make life easier and more enjoyable; for example, forests, water, and minerals

non-renewable resources—natural resources that disappear after being used; for example, gold and oil

O

ocean current—a stream of moving water within a larger body of water

organizer—a chart that helps show how information is related

outcrop—bedrock that is visible through the soil

P

peat—a deep layer of decaying plant life formed in wet conditions

peninsula—a piece of land surrounded by water on three sides

permafrost—ground that remains frozen all year round

physical features—the landforms, rivers, and lakes found in the area

physical region—an area that has similar physical characteristics throughout, such as landforms, climate, vegetation, and resources

picture graph—a visual way of organizing numerical (number) information; a legend is provided to show the amount each picture represents

political region—a place or area that has an agreed-upon boundary and its own government

precipitation—moisture that falls in the form of rain, snow, sleet, or hail, measured as centimetres of water

province—a major political division in Canada

provincial—having to do with a major political region within a country

public transportation—all of the ways to travel someplace that people pay to use in groups (not their own automobile)

R

raw materials—natural resources that are processed or refined by industries; industries change the natural resources into a different, more useful state

region—an area that is similar throughout and different from the places around it

relief map—a map that uses colour to represent elevation and show what the surface of the land is like; it may use some symbols

renewable resources—natural resources that do not disappear after being used because more are produced; for example, forests

S

scale—the relationship between distance measured on a map and the real distance on the Earth's surface

sedimentary rock—rock made from many layers of sediment that settled on top of each other and, over time, hardened into stone

services—groups or individuals who do something that is needed by others

softwood—the easy-to-cut wood of a coniferous tree

T

territory—a political region where control is shared between the territorial and the federal governments

theory—an idea that scientists believe to be true because there is a great deal of evidence, but it has not been proven

tides—changes in the level of the water that are caused by the pull of the Moon's gravity

transportation—moving people and goods from one place to another

treeline—an imaginary line beyond which trees can no longer grow; for example, trees cannot grow high on mountain tops or in the far North

tundra—large areas of treeless plain in the far North; tundra vegetation includes low shrubs, small plants, and mosses

V

vegetation—the plants that naturally grow in a region

W

wetlands—lands that are covered with water all or most of the time

Index

Arctic Ocean

N
W   E
S

YUKON

NORTHWEST
TERRITORIES

NUNA

Pacific
Ocean

BRITISH
COLUMBIA

ALBERTA

SASKATCHEWAN

MANITOB

Canada